Praise for *The Bible Questions*

"Hal Seed has given us all a great gift. His new book makes the Book more accessible to us all. If you have any questions about the Bible—this is the place to start."

JOHN ORTBERG, senior pastor of Menlo Park Presbyterian Church and author of *Who Is This Man?*

"I have read and studied the Bible many times over my fifty-plus years of ministry. But as I read *The Bible Questions,* I found myself saying over and over, 'I didn't know that!' *The Bible Questions* is well written, simple, short but thorough, and a practical guide for study by a small group or an individual. I recommend the book for the beginner or the longtime Christian who wants to learn more about the Bible."

BILL EASUM, president of 21st Century Strategies

"In *The Bible Questions,* Hal Seed sheds light on all aspects of what God intends for us with the Bible and how we can study it more effectively. Because he is a scholar as well as a teacher and practicing church leader, I cannot imagine a better all-around book for anything from a comprehensive church sermon series to a personal learning experience for Christians anywhere and everywhere!"

BIL CORNELIUS, founding pastor of Bay Area Fellowship and author of *I Dare You to Change!*

"*The Bible Questions* serves as a timely guide to the timeless Scriptures. New believers to aspiring theologians will appreciate its depth and simplicity. If you are looking for one book that combines academic scholarship along with practical application, this book is for you."

ERIC SWANSON, missional specialist for Leadership Network and coauthor of *The Externally Focused Church*

THE BIBLE QUESTIONS

Shedding Light on the World's Most Important Book

HAL SEED

IVP Books

An imprint of InterVarsity Press
Downers Grove, Illinois

InterVarsity Press
P.O. Box 1400, Downers Grove, IL 60515-1426
World Wide Web: www.ivpress.com
E-mail: email@ivpress.com

InterVarsity Press® is the book-publishing division of InterVarsity Christian Fellowship/USA®, a movement of students and faculty active on campus at hundreds of universities, colleges and schools of nursing in the United States of America, and a member movement of the International Fellowship of Evangelical Students. For information about local and regional activities, write Public Relations Dept., InterVarsity Christian Fellowship/USA, 6400 Schroeder Rd., P.O. Box 7895, Madison, WI 53707-7895, or visit the IVCF website at <www.intervarsity.org>.

All Scripture quotations, unless otherwise indicated, are taken from the Holy Bible, New International Version®, NIV® Copyright © 1973, 1978, 1984, 2011 by Biblica, Inc.™ Used by permission. All rights reserved worldwide.

While all stories in this book are true, some names and identifying information in this book have been changed to protect the privacy of the individuals involved.

Cover design: Cindy Kiple
Interior design: Beth Hagenberg
Images: old Bible: © Janet Hastings/iStockphoto
       bookmarks: © Ines Koleva/iStockphoto
       book with colorful tags: © Handan Yilmaz/iStockphoto

ISBN 978-0-8308-5612-1

Printed in the United States of America ∞

Library of Congress Cataloging-in-Publication Data

Seed, Hal, 1957-
   The Bible questions : shedding light on the world's most important
book / Hal Seed.
      p. cm.
   Includes bibliographical references.
   ISBN 978-0-8308-5612-1 (pbk. : alk. paper)
   1. Bible—Introductions. 2. Bible—Miscellanea. I. Title.

BS475.3.S44 2012
   220.6'1—dc23

                                                              2012018656

P	18	17	16	15	14	13	12	11	10	9	8	7	6	5	4	3	2	1
Y	27	26	25	24	23	22	21	20	19	18	17	16	15	14	13	12

The Bible Questions *is dedicated to you.*

God has written a book designed to make you into a magnificent example of what a human being ought to be. He took centuries to craft it, sewing into it his best thoughts for you and about you. He delights in turning its pages with you. Sometimes he'll shout to you from the text. Other times, he'll whisper. Listen carefully as you read and you will hear his voice speaking directly to you.

His words are living and active. As you read them, they will read you. I hope what I have written in this little book will in some small way encourage you to be read by God's book.

Contents

Foreword

◆ ◆ ◆

On every level of humanity, there is a deep yearning within us. We want to know more than what we can see and understand at face value. And on no other platform do we encounter more questions than in the confines of faith—questions that stem from our profound longing to further grasp what my good friend Hal Seed refers to as "the bigger picture of God and the Bible."

Every one of us seeks answers to the questions that arise from our beliefs. We thirst for understanding, development and maturity. Most people would openly admit that their greatest desire in reading the Bible is not just to *know* something but to be *known by someone.* When we admit this, we arrive at a place where answers are found; but more than that, an intimate, fulfilling and lifelong relationship with God is discovered. This process of discovery is the ultimate goal of not just the Bible, but also Hal's book *The Bible Questions.*

The Bible Questions is more than simply a reference book or study guide. It's a deeply thought-provoking and theologically sound manuscript that leads you through a historical journey and helps you discover the tools to answer some of the most poignant and philosophical questions we have asked since the beginning of our existence. *The Bible Questions* provides the fundamental keys to helping us answer the *what, why* and *how* of our own story with God.

Through meticulous detail of historical facts and brilliantly in-spired personal insight, Hal invites readers to begin to experience the Bible for themselves and unlock the incredible wisdom and practical knowledge found within. As a pastor and friend, I thank God for Hal's theological and doctrinal strength and for his com-mitment to help people think accurately about God.

As you make your way through this book, see it as a journey toward a greater sense of honor and reverence for the authenticity and authority of the Bible. Commit to give your best, and I believe God will give you his best through every revelation in his Word. Begin today to unlock the mysteries of the greatest book in history as you turn the page and answer *The Bible Questions.*

Come on somebody!

SERGIO DE LA MORA
Lead pastor, Cornerstone Church of San Diego
Author, *The Heart Revolution*

This Is the Bible

◆ ◆ ◆

The story of Vince Lombardi's opening-day practice with the Green Bay Packers is legendary. As the players assembled, Lombardi scanned the men, half his age and twice his size. The great coach walked to the front of the room, stood in silence for several seconds and then began. "Gentlemen," he said, "this is a football."

What Lombardi communicated that day led to five championships in nine years. The coach's point was, *If you're going to play football, you better know what a football is.*

The Bible is arguably the most important book ever written. It has influenced more lives, in more ways, than any other book in history. The Bible claims to be a key to understanding life. More than that, it claims to be able to guide you in living that life. If that's true, it's the most basic tool a person can possess.

Yet, everyone has questions about the Bible. At some point, they pick one up and wonder, where did this thing come from? Is it really true? Did God really write it? Can it really make my life better, or will it just trip me up and make my life boring?

Once they've read through it, they have more questions. Some are probing: *Did Jesus really walk on water? Did Moses really speak face-to-face with God?* Some are inquisitive: *Where did Cain get his wife? Where did Melchizedek come from?* Some are practical: *What's the point of the Bible? How can I best learn what it has to say?*

The purpose of *The Bible Questions* is not to answer every question you have, but to tackle the big picture questions and point you to tools that will help you to understand and master the background of this book. The good news is, there are answers to every question you'll ever ask about this amazing document. Along the way, I hope to whet your appetite for a lifelong relationship with the greatest book in history.

The Bible Questions is laid out as a four-week learning experience. There are five chapters per section. We start with the basics and move to the practical. My intent is to help you develop a habit of interacting with the Bible every day. If you will attend church one day, read a chapter a day for five more days, and spend an evening with a small group, discussing what you're learning using the discussion guide at the back of the book every week for four weeks, you'll find you've developed a very helpful habit.

PART ONE

Primary Questions

No other book has influenced man and history as has the Bible; its influence is reflected in the works of artists, poets, statesmen, musicians, sculptors, and scientists.

Steven Kumar

1

Who Wrote the Bible?

A man has deprived himself of the best there is in the world
who has deprived himself of a knowledge of the Bible.

Woodrow Wilson

♦ ♦ ♦

Before I read a new book, I always want to know who wrote it.
After all, an author's background and bias, interests and agenda,
will have tremendous influence on the contents of his or her
writing. So the most basic Bible question is, who wrote it?

BIBLE BASICS

I love it when friends pick up a Bible for the first time. They discover
a world they never knew existed. The opening chapters of Genesis
describe a perfect world. Then there's the Fall that destroyed paradise. Followed by God's rebuilding, which continues to this day.
The Bible is like no other book ever written. It's the story of God and
the history of the development of humanity. When people pick up a
Bible, they discover *their* story in a way they never knew it before.

The Bible was written long ago, in foreign lands, languages
and cultures. Some of it is hard to understand. Mark Twain said,
"It's not the parts of the Bible I can't understand that bother me,

it's the parts that I do understand." This is a book that reads *you* while you're reading it.

Maybe the most striking thing about the Bible is, people who begin reading it never stop reading it. My grandmother was introduced to a Bible as soon as she could read. At ninety-one she had a Bible with her at the hospital. In her final moments we recited Psalm 23 together.

My experience with the Bible started in my early teenage years. I laughed at a friend who said he'd been talking with God that morning. The idea seemed ridiculous to me. Then I attended a Christian coffee house meeting with him. I opened a Bible for the first time at that meeting. It was a borrowed Bible. The next morning I asked for a Bible for my birthday. Since that day, not a week has gone by that I haven't read some portion of Scripture and grown from it.

QUESTIONS

Everyone who reads the Bible has questions about it. Heck, everyone who has *heard* of the Bible has questions about it. Throughout these next twenty chapters, I'll do my best to answer the biggest and most frequently asked questions for you. My goal and purpose is not to answer detailed questions on specific passages. Those are important, so I'll point you to tools that can do that for you. My purpose here is to give you a broad and big picture understanding of what the Bible is all about, how it came into existence, and how to get the most out of it so that when you finish you'll have a love for the Bible. Toward the end of the book, I'll show you how to read the Bible in a way that will improve your life daily. It might just be that when you finish *The Bible Questions* you will find yourself starting a lifelong adventure in the most important book ever written.

Throughout the ages Christians have valued the Bible so highly that every theory, every controversy and every potential controversy has been documented and discussed in hundreds of books. Everything that's countable, quantifiable or identifiable has been published multiple times. I admit, I like studying those types of details. But that's not what *The Bible Questions* is about. This isn't a scholarly work. It's for people who have questions about the Bible. I want you to read ten to fifteen minutes a day for the next twenty days, then close the book and say, "I get it! I understand what the Bible is, what it's about and where it came from. And now I want to read it for myself!"

At the end of each chapter I'll ask you to spend five minutes on a short passage of Scripture. People who are in a hurry will be tempted to skip this assignment. Don't. I believe you'll find this the most helpful part of our experience together.

HOW THE BIBLE IS LAID OUT

The word *Bible* comes from the Greek word *biblos*, which means "book." The Bible has been such an important part of Christian history that those who read it find themselves simply calling it "the Book."

Yet the Bible is more than a book. It's a book of books. It's a compilation of sixty-six different books written over a period of fifteen hundred years by more than forty writers. These writers came from over twenty different occupations, wrote in a variety of moods, in three different languages, from ten different countries, on three different continents, with a consistency of message and without contradictions.[1]

Open a Bible to its table of contents and you'll find this:

OLD TESTAMENT

Genesis	2 Chronicles	Daniel
Exodus	Ezra	Hosea
Leviticus	Nehemiah	Joel
Numbers	Esther	Amos
Deuteronomy	Job	Obadiah
Joshua	Psalms	Jonah
Judges	Proverbs	Micah
Ruth	Ecclesiastes	Nahum
1 Samuel	Song of Songs	Habakkuk
2 Samuel	Isaiah	Zephaniah
1 Kings	Jeremiah	Haggai
2 Kings	Lamentations	Zechariah
1 Chronicles	Ezekiel	Malachi

NEW TESTAMENT

Matthew	Ephesians	Hebrews
Mark	Philippians	James
Luke	Colossians	1 Peter
John	1 Thessalonians	2 Peter
Acts	2 Thessalonians	1 John
Romans	1 Timothy	2 John
1 Corinthians	2 Timothy	3 John
2 Corinthians	Titus	Jude
Galatians	Philemon	Revelation

The Old Testament. The books of the Old Testament are arranged by *type* of literature. The first five books are called the Books of Moses. Together with the next twelve (Genesis through Esther), they form the *historical* section of the Old Testament. The succeeding five books (Job through Song of Songs) are the *poetical* section. The final seventeen books (Isaiah through Malachi) are the *prophetical* section.

The books of Moses. Raised and educated in the courts of Pharaoh, Moses was uniquely qualified to research and record the earliest history of the world and the early history of the Hebrew people. Moses' writings are so important to the Jews they refer to his five books as "the Law."

There is scholarly debate surrounding the date of the exodus, but according to tradition, around 1446 B.C., Moses emancipated the Hebrews from slavery in Egypt and led them to Mount Sinai. There God invited Moses to the top of the mountain for a spiritual conversation. Moses and his apprentice, Joshua, climbed Mount Sinai and spent the next forty days listening to God.

This was a seminal moment in human history. God had spoken to others before, but never in such detail and with such specific directions about how he wanted his people to live. At the end of their meeting, God handed Moses two stone tablets on which he had inscribed ten words with his own finger. Those words have become known as "the Ten Commandments."

Those two stone tablets may have been the first portions of Scripture ever written. Moses spent the next forty years giving context to God's words. According to tradition, he gathered sources and collected oral accounts that enabled him to preface God's commandments with a synopsis of earth's ancient history (Genesis 1–11). He recorded the stories of his own ancestors over the previous three hundred years (Genesis 12–50). As a prince of Egypt, it's hard to imagine anyone better prepared to understand and integrate all the available records, manuscripts and oral traditions that went into writing the book of Genesis.

Next came the books of Exodus, Numbers, Leviticus and Deuteronomy. These are accounts of Israel's wilderness wanderings, the lessons they learned there, and God's directions for how to live. The final chapter of Deuteronomy describes Moses' death and burial. Since Moses couldn't have written it himself, scholars believe this twelve-verse epitaph was written by Joshua in honor of his lifelong mentor.

One of Moses' final instructions to the people was, "Take this Book of the Law and place it beside the ark of the covenant of the LORD your God" (Deuteronomy 31:26). The ark became the collecting place for sacred Scripture. If you've seen *Raiders of the Lost Ark*, you know that the ark of the covenant was a sacred, decorative box that was kept in the Israelites' tabernacle. Later, when King Solomon built the temple in Jerusalem, the ark (and presumably all the scrolls of Scripture) was transferred there. In chapter four we'll discover how meticulously the Jews kept and cared for these scrolls. From their earliest history the Israelites believed that as they handled the books of Moses, they were handling the very words of God.

The other historical books. Upon Moses' death, Israel's leadership transferred to Joshua. Joshua led the people in conquering the land of Canaan and settling it as their permanent home. Joshua recorded history while he was making it. Fittingly, the Israelites called the book he wrote "Joshua." Three small portions (Joshua 15:13-19; 19:47; 24:29-33) were likely inserted by Phinehas, the high priest of Israel, soon after Joshua's death.

Joshua is the first of what has been not-so-creatively called "the other historical books." This section of the Bible records Israel's rise to nationhood, superpower status under King David, the division of the kingdom into the two kingdoms, the conquest of each by foreign powers, and the miraculous return of the nation of Judah following exile in Babylon. These historical records demonstrate God's love and patience with his people, and give us the backdrop we need for understanding the questions and answers posed in the poetical section, along with the messages delivered in the prophetical section.

The Bible says that Samuel wrote "on a scroll and deposited it before the LORD" (1 Samuel 10:25). The Talmud, which is the authoritative Jewish commentary on the Old Testament, credits Samuel with writing the books of Judges, Ruth and most of 1 Samuel.

Samuel established a school of prophets (1 Samuel 10:5; 19:20), who carried on his work of recording the history of God's people. These writers included Nathan, Gad, Ahijah, Iddo, Jehu and Isaiah.[2] One or all of these writers composed the remainder of 1 Samuel and all of 2 Samuel.

We believe the prophet Jeremiah compiled the books of 1-2 Kings. Within them he cites "The Book of the Acts of Solomon," "The Book of the Chronicles of the Kings of Israel" and "The Book of the Chronicles of the Kings of Judah"[3] as sources he used to reconstruct the four hundred years of Israel's kingdom period. Jeremiah also wrote the book of Lamentations. With the help of a scribe named Baruch (Jeremiah 36:18; 45:1) he also wrote the book that bears his name.

The Talmud tells us that Ezra the Scribe authored the books of Chronicles. First and Second Chronicles are a selective account of Israel's history, written for the benefit of the Israelites who returned from exile in Babylon.[4] Ezra also wrote the book that bears his name, and he probably wrote, or helped write, the book of Nehemiah, using Nehemiah's personal journal.

The poetical books. You see an instant transition when you turn the page from the historical to the poetical books. The most obvious difference is that Job, Psalms, Proverbs, Ecclesiastes and Songs were written in poetic form rather than prose. Their purpose is different. The poetical books are called "wisdom literature" because they offer words and sayings designed to make us wise. They answer deep questions of the heart and soul. Questions like

- Why is there so much suffering in this world? (Job)

- How can I express my inner feelings to God? (Psalms)

- How do I make great choices? (Proverbs)

- What's the point of life? (Ecclesiastes)

- How can a man and woman really love each other? (Songs)

It's likely that the earliest recorded Scripture is the book of Job. A Talmudic tradition suggests that Moses wrote Job, which is debatable. Job's story takes place in the land of Uz, which was next door to Midian, Moses' adopted homeland. It's possible Moses heard the story told around campfires and recorded it for posterity.

Job himself, or his friend Elihu, may also have written the book. If that's true, the book could have been written as early as 1900 B.C. Job's life and lifestyle are similar to that of Abraham, who lived during that time period. Like Abraham, Job's wealth was measured in livestock (Job 1:3; 42:12) rather than gold and silver. Like Abraham, Job was the priest of his family and offered sacrifices, something forbidden after the law was introduced by Moses. Job makes no references to the nation of Israel, the exodus, the Mosaic law or the tabernacle. And the Chaldeans who murdered Job's servants (Job 1:17) were nomadic raiders, not the city dwellers they became in centuries that followed.

Because the book of Job seems to be written as a drama, some say that Job was a character in a play rather than a real, live person. Ezekiel 14:14 and James 5:11 indicate that Job was real, so I tend to believe he actually lived. Job's authorship will remain a mystery until we get to heaven.

Psalms is the songbook of Israel, written by people from every walk of life. King Dave wrote seventy-five of them.[5] King Solomon wrote two (Psalm 72; 127). Moses contributed Psalm 90. Twelve were authored by a temple musician named Asaph (Psalm 50; 73–83), one came from a musician named Heman (Psalm 88). Ten were composed by a group of temple gatekeepers called "the sons of Korah" (Psalm 42; 44–49; 84–85; 87). Fifty are anonymous. Tradition has it that the priest Ezra may have written a few of these.

Most, if not all, of the book of Proverbs was written by Solomon, who is said to be the wisest man who ever lived. According to 1 Kings 4:32, "he spoke three thousand proverbs and his songs numbered a thousand and five." Chapter headings tell us that Agur wrote chapter 30, and King Lemuel wrote chapter 31. Some believe these may be nicknames for Solomon himself.

Solomon also wrote the book of Ecclesiastes, with editorial work done by scribes in the days of Hezekiah (Proverbs 25:1). Song of Songs is also called the Song of Solomon, so we don't have to wander far to figure out its author.

The prophetical books. The seventeen books of the prophetical section are some of the most challenging in the entire Bible. Many of them use figures of speech that can be hard to figure out by Western, twenty-first-century readers. I recommend reading these books with the help of a commentary so you can understand why each prophet wrote what he did, and the meaning of each geographic and cultural reference.

The New Testament. The New Testament is also divided into

three sections. Its first five books are historical, followed by twenty-two books called epistles.

A Sunday school class was once asked, "What are epistles?"

One little boy answered, "They're the wives of the apostles."

Not quite!

The biblical epistles are letters written by the apostles to young churches during the first fifty years after Jesus' ascension, from about A.D. 46 to 80 or 90. The final book of the New Testament is the prophetical book of Revelation.

Historical books. The first four New Testament books are the Gospels. *Gospel* is an Old English word that means "good news." These four books were written by Matthew, Mark, Luke and John. Matthew was one of Jesus' original twelve disciples. Mark was a disciple of both Peter and Paul, and probably also Barnabas's nephew. Luke was a medical doctor who accompanied Paul on his missionary journeys. He is the only Gentile author of a biblical book, and he wrote two of them: the books of Luke and Acts. Acts is actually a continuation of the story Luke began in his Gospel. Acts tells what happens to the people of God after Jesus' resurrection. It's the story of the beginnings of the church.

The books of Matthew, Mark and Luke are called the *Synoptic Gospels*. *Synoptic* is a Greek word that means "to see with the same eyes." These three books largely tell the same stories, sometimes with exactly the same words. Theory has it that Mark wrote the earliest Gospel using material he learned from Peter. Soon after his work was done, Matthew and Luke used Mark's Gospel as one of their resources when writing their accounts.

John was the youngest of Jesus' twelve apostles and outlived the rest. As the last living eyewitness to the life of Christ, John knew miracles and stories that no one would know unless he wrote them down. Aware of the material already covered by the Synoptic Gospels, John wrote what has been called a supplemental Gospel. John records his own perspective on the stories of the feeding of the five thousand, the Last Supper, the crucifixion and the resurrection, which are also found in the Synoptics. The rest of his material is unique, supplementing what was told by Matthew, Mark and Luke.

Paul's epistles. The apostle Paul wrote thirteen of the twenty-two letters of the New Testament (Romans through Philemon).

The other letters. No one knows for sure who wrote the book of Hebrews. Some believe it was a sermon preached by Paul. Others think it was written by a church planter named Apollos (Acts 18:24). One intriguing theory suggests it was written by Priscilla, a female leader in the church, who did not identify herself in order to keep the book from gender bias.

The epistle of James was written by one of Jesus' half-brothers. Its pithy sayings have caused people to call it the New Testament book of Proverbs.

The apostle Peter wrote his two letters to encourage Christians who were suffering for the cause of Christ. John wrote 1 John to warn Christians about the Gnostic heresy that was beginning to develop. He wrote 2 John to a lady and her children, and 3 John to a man named Gaius. These letters may have been personal notes or "cover letters" to accompany the letter of 1 John.

Jude was written by a second of Jesus' half-brothers. Its apocryphal references make it a bit confusing. Like the Old Testament prophets, I recommend reading it with a commentary in hand. The same goes for the book of Revelation.

Revelation is John's record of a vision God gave him while he was in exile on the island of Patmos. The vision describes the future of the world, the return of Christ and the establishment of the new heavens and new earth.

ASSIGNMENT

The best way to both appreciate and understand the Bible is to read it for yourself. Open a Bible to Psalm 19 and read its fourteen short verses. While you're reading, answer the following questions:

1. Do you hear God speaking to you?

2. If so, what is he saying?

3. How does this psalm show you life as it really is?

2

How Is the Bible Different from Other Books?

The Bible is a book like no other.

Carol J. Ruvolo

♦ ♦ ♦

Most people have a perception that the Bible is different from all other books—and they are right. If there were a hall of fame for books, the Bible would qualify on the first ballot. No other piece of literature has its pedigree. Besides its all-star lineup of authors, the Bible heads the lists of world's firsts in many categories:

- First major book to be translated into a foreign language. In 250 B.C. the Old Testament of the Bible was translated from Hebrew to Greek. The translation is called the Septuagint, which is still available today.

- First true book to be printed in Europe.[1] In 1440, Johann Gutenberg, a diamond polisher, invented the printing press. By 1455 he and his colleagues had produced "The Gutenberg Bible."

- First book to be telegraphed. On May 24, 1844, Samuel Morse coded Numbers 23:23, "What hath God wrought!" (KJV) from the chamber of the U.S. Supreme Court to Albert Vail at the B & O Railroad depot in Baltimore, Maryland.

- First book on the moon. On July 20, 1969, before exiting the *Eagle* lunar space module, Buzz Aldrin pulled out a Bible, a silver chalice, and sacramental bread and wine. He read the Bible before putting a boot on the moon.

NO OTHER BOOK HAS BEEN SO ANTICIPATED

In its first print run of the New International Version of the Bible, the International Bible Society produced an initial printing of 1,200,000 Bibles, which sold out before making it to market. Apparently, a lot of people in the English-speaking world love the Bible.

We're not the only ones.

When Bruce Olson was nineteen years old, he left home for an adventure in the jungles of Colombia, South America. Bruce felt led to share the Bible with a tribe of seminomadic Stone Age indigenous people there called the Motilones (moe-til-oh-nees). After five years of learning their language and culture, Bruce discovered that these aggressive cannibals felt a tremendous sense of grief and loss because they had, "lost God's trail" and did not know how to find it so they could walk with him again.

One day, a Motilone named Arabadoyca told Bruce of their hope for finding God. "There is a prediction that a tall man with yellow hair will come with a banana stalk, and God will come out of the banana stalk,"[2] Arabadoyca said.

Not understanding, Bruce forgot about this conversation until the day he met a Motilone mourning the loss of his brother. In Bruce's own words, "This tribesman told me the story of the false prophet who had led them away from God. 'We no longer know God,' he said quietly."

A lively discussion started. The man reminded us of the legend about the prophet who would come carrying the banana stalks, and that God would come out of those stalks.

I couldn't quite understand that idea behind the legend. "Why look for God to come out of a banana stalk?" I asked.

There was a puzzled silence. It made sense to them, but they couldn't explain it. Bobby [Bruce's English nickname for his favorite Motilone] walked over to a banana tree which was growing nearby. He cut off a section and tossed it toward us.

"This is the kind of banana stalk God can come from," he said. It was a cross section from the stalk. It rolled at our feet.

One of the Motilones reached down and swatted at it with his machete, accidentally splitting it in half. One half stood up, while the other half split off. Leaves that were still inside the stalk, waiting to develop and come out, started peeling off. As they lay at the base of the stalk, they looked like pages from a book.

Suddenly a word raced through my mind, "Book! Book!"

I grabbed up my pack and took out my Bible. I opened it. Flipping through the pages, I held it toward the men. I pointed to the leaves from the banana stalk, then back to the Bible.

"This is it!" I said. "I have it here! This is God's banana stalk!"[3]

The Motilones embraced what Bruce taught them from "God's banana stalk." News that it had arrived spread from village to village. No other book has been anticipated like the Bible, and no other book has been received the way it has.

NO OTHER BOOK HAS BEEN SO RESISTED

Since its inception, the Bible has been burned and banished by more people and cultures than any other book. For centuries the only translation of the Bible available to the peoples of Europe was a fourth-century Latin translation called the Vulgate. Only priests and scholars knew Latin. The Church of Rome forbade translation into common languages for fear that the masses would misunderstand (or possibly, understand) the message of the Bible.

When William Tyndale (c. 1494-1536) became convinced that ordinary English people ought to be able to read the Bible for themselves, his life was threatened. He hid in Germany and Belgium while completing his work. After Tyndale's Bible was published, it was burned on the streets of London, and a bounty was placed on his head.

Tyndale was tried for heresy and strangled to death. His body was then burned for good measure. Tyndale's final words were "Lord! Open the King of England's eyes." Four years later, the king ordered not one but *four* English translations to be made. All of them were based on Tyndale's work.

NO OTHER BOOK HAS BEEN SO LOVED

The Bible is the bestselling book of all time. No other book comes close. The NIV (New International Version) *alone* has sold over 400 million copies. Most Christians own more than one. Many own even more. As I glance over my shoulder, I see no less than eighteen versions on my shelf, and I have more at my office at the church!

One of the unique aspects of the Bible is that people who begin to read it, never finish. They'll read its sixty-six books and then begin again. They'll read one chapter of the New Testament, and read it again the next day.

The Bible is so loved that it's been translated into more languages than any other book in history. As of 2011, it's estimated that there are less than 350,000 people who do not have a translation available in a language they understand.[4]

Biblica estimates that it takes twelve years for a team to translate the Bible into a new language. Like Bruce Olson, these translators pay a significant social and emotional price for their efforts, leaving families, friends and cultural conveniences to bring the Bible to others. They do this willingly, because they love the Bible and what it can do for people.

NO OTHER BOOK MAKES SUCH SUPERNATURAL CLAIMS

The Qur'an, Tripitaka, Bhagavad-Gita, and Book of Mormon claim divine oversight, but none make a combination of supernatural claims similar to the Bible.

- The Bible claims to be perfect: "The law of the LORD is perfect" (Psalm 19:7).

- It claims to be flawless: "Every word of God is flawless" (Proverbs 30:5).

- It claims to predict the future: "Write . . . what will take place later" (Revelation 1:19).

- It claims to judge our inmost thoughts: "[The word of God] judges the thoughts and attitudes of the heart" (Hebrews 4:12).

Making such claims may not be all that impressive, but backing them up certainly is. Let's look at the claim that can be most tangibly verified: can the Bible really predict the future?

J. Barton Payne's *Encyclopedia of Biblical Prophecy* lists 1,239 prophecies in the Old Testament and 578 prophecies in the New Testament, for a total of 1,817.[5] If even one of those prophecies does not come true, then the Bible is neither perfect nor flawless. So how does it do in fulfilling its own predictions?

Of those prophecies, Jesus fulfilled 332 prophecies in his first coming. In *The God Questions* I referenced a study done by mathematician Peter Stoner.[6] To see how likely it is that anyone or any book could fulfill so many predictions, Dr. Stoner calculated the odds of one person fulfilling eight of those prophecies at 1 in 100,000,000,000,000,000. If you filled the state of Texas two feet deep with silver dollars, they'd total that number. Imagine blindfolding someone and asking them to pick a specific coin on their first try. That's a 1 in 100,000,000,000,000,000 chance!

Stoner then calculated the odds of someone fulfilling forty-eight prophecies. That number was so large it was greater than the number of atoms in the universe.

In *Future History* I examine the fulfillment of prophecies in Daniel 11.[7] This one chapter of the Bible contains 135 prophecies that were all fulfilled between two hundred and four hundred years after Daniel recorded them.[8] The Bible is so good at fulfilling prophecy that antisupernaturalists believe the book of Daniel must have been written by someone many years after Daniel's death.

NO OTHER BOOK MAKES SUCH SIGNIFICANT PROMISES

Since the Bible is like no other book, it can deliver on promises like no other book. Here are just three of the many promises it makes:

- It promises wisdom to those who read it: "Your commands . . . make me wiser than my enemies" (Psalm 119:98).

- It promises insight to those who think about it: "I have more insight than all my teachers, / for I meditate on your statutes" (Psalm 119:99).

- It promises guidance to those who follow it: "Your word is a lamp for my feet, / a light on my path" (Psalm 119:105).

ASSIGNMENT

Psalm 119 is a tribute to the greatness of the Bible. It's an alphabetical psalm. The first eight verses each start with the letter *A* ("aleph" in Hebrew). The next eight begin with the letter *B* ("bet"). If you want to know the Hebrew alphabet, just look at the stanza headings of Psalm 119.

Read Psalm 119:97-105.

1. What do these verses say about the Bible?

2. What promises do you find here?

3. What does this passage cause you to want to do?

3

Who Decided
What Went into the Bible?

[The Bible is] built on the foundation of the apostles and prophets,
with Christ Jesus himself as the chief cornerstone.

The Apostle Paul, Ephesians 2:20

♦ ♦ ♦

Just about everyone wants to know how the sixty-six books got chosen to be in the Bible. Why these sixty-six? Why not a few more (or a few less)? Why these books and not others?

In *Persecution in the Early Church* Herbert Workman tells the story of a Christian who was brought before the Roman governor of Sicily during the last great persecution of the church. His crime? Possessing a copy of the Gospels.

The governor asked, "Where did these come from? Did you bring them from your home?"

The believer replied, "I have no home, as my Lord Jesus knows."

The governor asked his prisoner to read a portion of the Gospels. He chose a portion of Jesus' Sermon on the Mount: "Blessed are those who are persecuted because of righteousness, for theirs is the kingdom of heaven." Next he read from Luke: "If anyone would come after me, he must deny himself and take up his cross daily and follow me."

At this, the judge ordered the prisoner taken away—to his death.[1]

Under Roman law new religions were illegal. In its first few decades Christianity was seen as a sect within Judaism. Once it was determined that Christianity was a separate religion, it became illegal to identify as a Christian. So, for the first three centuries of what we now call the Christian Era, it was a crime to be Christian. Persecutions sprang up throughout various parts of the empire. Believers were tortured and sometimes martyred for their faith. In 303, Emperor Diocletian ordered the confiscation of Christian property and churches, and the burning of Scriptures. Believers and their Book had become so inseparable that the way to eliminate Christianity was to eliminate the Bible.

HOW THE BIBLE CAME TOGETHER

Who decided what went into the Bible? The short answer to that question is *no one*. Or maybe a better answer is *God did*. When scholars talk about how a book qualified to be called Scripture, they list five characteristics called the *laws of canonicity*. But these characteristics are *recognized* in hindsight; they weren't developed by a particular group at a particular time in history.

After his resurrection Jesus commissioned his followers to go and make disciples, and they did. They devoted themselves to sharing the Christ's good news, enfolding people into local churches and teaching them to obey all that Jesus had commanded.

These Jewish believers already had Scripture. Around Palestine the Jewish Scripture is exactly what Protestants today call the Old Testament. Jesus referred to these books when he spoke of the Law of Moses, the Prophets and the Psalms (Luke 24:44).

Outside the Holy Land some Jews included twelve to fifteen other books as part of Scripture. The Septuagint, which was translated in Egypt, contains books that we now call the Apocrypha.

(*Apocrypha* means "those hidden away.") Early Christians differed over whether these *extra* books should be considered Scripture or not. Those nearest Palestine tended to exclude them. Those closer to Rome tended to include them.

During the sixteenth-century Reformation, Martin Luther spoke strongly against the Apocrypha. In reaction the Roman Catholic Church convened a council in Trent (now in Italy), where they declared the Apocrypha to be canonical. To this day Catholics and Protestants disagree on this issue. Catholics uphold the Apocrypha. Protestants believe that the Apocrypha is useful but not inspired.

Wherever Christianity spread, Christians gathered for worship and instruction. In keeping with the customs of the Jewish synagogue, a portion of Old Testament Scripture would be read and explained. Meanwhile, the apostles, along with other evangelists and teachers, traveled from place to place to plant churches and encourage believers. When one of these recognized leaders was in town, he was invited to speak during the service.

As need arose, the apostles wrote letters to various churches. When a letter arrived, it was read with great excitement in the worship service. Often the letter would be copied and shared with neighboring churches, who, in turn, would share it with still other churches. Naturally, the more inspiring letters were copied and shared more often.

In his letter to the Colossians, Paul wrote, "After this letter has been read to you, see that it is also read in the church of the Laodiceans and that you in turn read the letter from Laodicea" (Colossians 4:16). We still have the letter to the Colossians. The letter to the Laodiceans was not considered inspired or pertinent enough to be preserved.

Around A.D. 150, Justin Martyr described worship this way:

> On the day called the Day of the Sun all who live in cities or in the country gather together to one place, and the memoirs

of the apostles or the writings of the prophets are read, as long as time permits; then, when the reader has ceased, the president verbally instructs, and exhorts to the imitation of these good things. Then all rise together and pray.[2]

By this early date, "the memoirs of the apostles" were considered as important to the teaching of the church as the writings of the prophets.

Marcion and Montanus. About ten years earlier a wealthy ship owner named Marcion sailed from his home near the Black Sea to the capital city of Rome. Marcion believed that the God of the Old Testament was different than the God of the New Testament. The former was distant and loved justice, while the latter was loving and emphasized grace.

Marcion rejected the Old Testament, along with any writings that might reinforce views other than his own. He developed a list of books he considered acceptable: portions of the Gospel of Luke, ten of Paul's letters, plus a letter purportedly from Paul to the Alexandrians. This list is known as the Marcion Canon.

The church had to respond to this. Though nothing had been officially written down, decided or proclaimed, most Christians had a sense of what was Scripture and what wasn't.

Between A.D. 156 and 172, a second provocateur appeared on the scene. His name was Montanus. Montanus was accompanied by two prophetesses, Prisca and Maximilla. "The Three" spoke in ecstatic visions and encouraged their followers to fast and pray, calling the church to a higher standard of righteousness and zeal. If that was as far as their teaching went, they would have been an asset. But their message included what they called "new prophecy," which pushed Christ and the apostolic message into the background. The age of Jesus was being superseded by the age of the Holy Spirit, and Montanus was its spokesman.

Was Montanus truly bringing a new prophecy with new authority? Prophecy more authoritative than Jesus and the apostles? This question prompted the church to respond a second time.

In A.D. 144, the church of Rome excommunicated Marcion and continued the sifting process on what was Scripture and what wasn't. The Montanus controversy pushed the church to ask further questions of their Scriptures. Specifically, was God bringing further revelation? Could that revelation be true if it contradicted things taught by Jesus and the apostles? Could new truth change or add to the basic teachings the church had been feeding on for the past century? The answer was no. From this the church concluded that the canon of Scripture was closed.

Spurred by these dilemmas the church developed its list of canonical books. The following are guidelines for accepting a book into the New Testament:

1. Was the book written by a prophet of God?

2. Was the writer confirmed by acts of God?

3. Does the message tell the truth about God?

4. Did it come with the power of God?

5. Was it accepted by God's people?[3]

These are the *marks of canonicity.* "Canon" is a Greek word meaning "rule" or "measuring stick." These five questions are used to determine which books "measure up" to being labeled divinely inspired. They exhibit "the marks of canonicity."

Turn to a Bible's table of contents and you'll see that each of the books was written by either a prophet or apostle (Ephesians 2:20), or by someone with a direct relationship to one.

Miracles were the means by which God confirmed the authority of his spokesmen. In Exodus 4, Moses was given miraculous powers to confirm his call. In 2 Corinthians 12:12, Paul teaches that the mark of an apostle is "signs, wonders and miracles."

Truth cannot contradict itself, so agreement with the other

books of Scripture was only logical. As was historical accuracy. If the facts of a book were inaccurate, it couldn't have been from God.

The inner witness of the Spirit was equally important. A key question these early Christians asked was, When we read this, is there an inner sense from God that what is written is right and true?

Initial acceptance by people to whom the work was addressed was crucial. What was the original audience's sense? Did they accept the book as an authoritative word from God? Daniel, who lived within a few years of Jeremiah, called Jeremiah's book "Scripture" in Daniel 9:2. Paul called the Gospel of Luke "Scripture" in 1 Timothy 5:18. Peter affirmed that Paul's letters were "Scripture" in 2 Peter 3:16.

The Muratorian Fragment. Even before Marcion and Montanus, the church was aware of these important criteria. In A.D. 96, Clement of Rome wrote "The apostles were made evangelists to us by the Lord Christ; Jesus Christ was sent by God. Thus Christ is from God and the apostles from Christ. . . . The Church is built on them as a foundation" (1 Clement 42).

After Marcion and Montanus, lists of New Testament books begin to appear. One of the first was The Muratorian Fragment. It was discovered among the Vatican's sacred documents by historian Ludovico Antonio Muratori in 1740 and dates to about A.D. 190. The fragment is damaged. The portion we possess begins with "the third book of the Gospel is that according to Luke." We assume the first and second Gospels to be Matthew and Mark. The fragment lists John, Acts, all of Paul's letters, James, 1-2 John, Jude and the Revelation of John. It also includes the Revelation of Peter, the Wisdom of Solomon and ("to be used in private, but not public worship") the Shepherd of Hermas.

Eusebius. By the early third century only a handful of books that we now call our New Testament were in question. In western regions of the empire, the book of Hebrews faced opposition, and in the east Revelation was unpopular. Eusebius, a church historian of the fourth century, records that James, 2 Peter, 2-3 John and Jude were the only books "spoken against" (though recognized by others).

Athanasius. In 367, Athanasius, the bishop of Alexandria, wrote an Easter letter that contained all twenty-seven books of our present New Testament. In 393 the Synod of Hippo affirmed our current New Testament, and in 397 the Council of Carthage published the same list.

WHO DECIDED WHAT BELONGS IN THE CANON?

Theologians are careful to note that the church didn't develop the canon, God did that by inspiring its writing and superintending each book's preservation. The church *recognized* the canon by experience and mutual agreement.

ASSIGNMENT

Read 2 Peter 1:19-21.

1. What is "the prophetic message as something completely reliable"?

2. What are we supposed to do with "the prophetic message"?

3. Where did the prophecies of Scripture come from?

4. What does chapter three of *The Bible Questions* make you want to do?

4

How Accurate Is the Bible?

*The Christian can take the whole Bible in his hand and say
without fear or hesitation that he holds in it the true Word of God,
handed down without essential loss from generation
to generation throughout the centuries.*

Sir Frederic Kenyon

◆ ◆ ◆

One of the most frequently asked Bible questions is, The book is so old and has been copied so many times, from one language to another, how can we really know what it originally said?

Part of the answer is, the Bible *hasn't* been copied all that much. Yes, we have thousands of copies, but the Bible wasn't copied hastily, and it wasn't copied from language A to language B to language C to language D. It's not like the game of telephone, where a message is passed from person to person with increasing distortion. When Bible scholars produce new editions or translations today, they work straight from the original languages of Hebrew and Greek, with surprising sophistication and clarity.

A few years ago I was training church leaders in London. We had one free day and my wife, Lori, and I used it to go sightseeing. We took in all the big attractions: Buckingham Palace, Westminster Abbey, the River Thames. But the thing I most wanted to see was inside the British Library.

The British Library ought to be declared one of the seven wonders of the modern world. Not only is it free, but it also contains some of the most important literary works of history. In a special section called "the Treasures," it houses the complete works of Shakespeare and original copies of *Alice in Wonderland*, *Winnie the Pooh* and (my wife's favorite) *Jane Eyre*. It has original Mozart manuscripts, two of the four existing copies of the Magna Carta, Leonardo da Vinci's notebook and more. They're kept under glass, carefully preserved for all to see. Every time Lori and I leaned down to examine one, we felt like we were touching history.

Not far from these marvels is the prize I came for. It's called Codex Sinaiticus. One of the two oldest Bibles in the world.

CODEX SINAITICUS

Sinaiticus (sin-ay-it-eh-cus) is only one copy of the Scriptures, but what we know of it demonstrates the amount of attention that has gone into copying and preserving the Bible as a whole.

Sinaiticus is a 1,460-page copy of the Bible in Greek. It's made of parchment, the skin of animals, in this case, mostly very young cows. Sinaiticus's parchment is thin and smooth, which means great care went into selecting the specific hides that would become pages (or leaves) of the document. Producing Sinaiticus was expensive. Whoever commissioned it must have been a person of means.

From the handwriting as well as the markings at the end of each book, we know that a team of four scribes worked on the text. All of them were trained with the same deliberate strokes so that the words appear uniform, as if they'd been printed. Each scribe corrected his own work, and one of them corrected and revised parts by another.

Juan Garces, curator of the British Library Codex Sinaiticus Project, says, "It had to be planned very carefully, because you would need to know almost from the beginning how many leaves you would use, how they would be gathered into quires, . . . and how they would be bound at the very end."[1]

Emperor Constantine legalized Christianity in A.D. 313. In 331 he commissioned fifty copies of the Bible to be produced at government expense. Curators at the British Library date Sinaiticus to about A.D. 350. Sinaiticus represents a leap forward in technology. Before this date, individual books of the Bible were copied into much smaller volumes. This may be the first bound book ever produced.

Sinaiticus was discovered by Constantin von Tischendorf at the Monastery of St. Catherine, near the base of Mount Sinai, in 1844. Since St. Catherine is a Russian Orthodox monastery, Tischendorf convinced the monks there to loan the documents to the Czar of Russia. In 1933, Joseph Stalin sold a portion of it to the British Library. The British have since worked to unite the entire manuscript and will soon make it available for viewing online.

THE NEW TESTAMENT

The care and detail that went into the production of Sinaiticus and its preservation, documentation and reproduction today is reflective of how the Bible has been handled throughout its history. For the past two thousand years, Christians have believed that when they hold the Bible in their hands, they hold the very words of God. So they treat it accordingly.

Were errors ever made in copying the New Testament? Most definitely. Fortunately, we have more than 5,300 ancient copies of the Greek New Testament, 10,000 copies of the Latin translation and more than 9,300 copies in other ancient languages—24,000 manuscripts in all. This means that when a scholar or translator wants to determine the most likely wording of the original text, he or she has a mountain of documents to consult.

Compare the New Testament's 24,000 copies to the second-best preserved work of history, Homer's *Iliad*, which boasts 643 copies, and the Bible is hands down the most textually accurate document in history. Of the entire New Testament, only four hundred words (0.5 percent) are in question. The variants of these words are so slight that no doctrine of Christianity is affected by the potential alterations in meaning.[2]

THE OLD TESTAMENT

If anything, the Jewish scribes who superintended the Old Testament were even more meticulous than their New Testament counterparts.

The Talmudists were scribes put in charge of copying and caring for the Jews' holy texts from A.D. 100 to 500. According to their rules, synagogue scrolls had to be written on specifically prepared skins of clean animals. Each skin had to contain a specific number of columns. Each column had to be between forty-eight and sixty lines, and thirty letters wide. The spacing between consonants, sections and books was precise, measured by hairs or threads. The ink had to be black, from a specific recipe. The transcriber could not deviate from the text in any manner. No word could be written from memory. Each copyist had to wash his body, work in full Jewish dress and not write the name of God with a pen newly dipped in ink. Their official mandate was, "And should a king address him while writing that name, he must take no notice of him."[3]

A second group, called the Masoretes oversaw the text from A.D. 500 to 900. The Masoretes numbered the verses, words and letters of each book and calculated the midpoint of each one. When a scroll was complete, independent sources counted the number of words and syllables forward, backward and from the middle of the text in each direction. Proofreading and revision had to be done within thirty days of a completed manuscript. Two mistakes per page could be corrected. Three mistakes on a page condemned the whole manuscript.

THE DEAD SEA SCROLLS

The Jews held their sacred writings in such high regard that they rarely let them get old or faded. Custom dictated that worn manuscripts be buried or burned. Unlike the New Testament, where we have thousands of ancient manuscripts to compare, there are few ancient manuscripts of the Hebrew Old Testament. Until 1947, our most aged manuscripts dated from the ninth century A.D.

Fortunately, a discovery was made in 1947 that changed everything. In March of that year a young Bedouin boy named Muhammed edh-Dhib was looking for a lost goat about a mile from the Dead Sea. To ward off other animals, he threw a rock into a cave that has now become known as Cave 1 of Qumran.

Every country bordering Israel gets its wealth from oil. Israel's wealth comes from technology and archaeology. When Muhammed edh-Dhib heard the sound of breaking pottery, he instinctively went to investigate. What he found was perhaps the richest biblical treasure ever discovered.

Cave 1 housed several large jars with rolls of leather and papyrus wrapped in cloth. Muhammed brought them to an antique dealer in Bethlehem. The antique dealer contacted a Syrian scholar, who stored several manuscripts at the Monastery of St. Mark in Jerusalem. When Professor Eleazar Lipa Sukenik of Hebrew University saw them he said, "This may be one of the greatest finds ever made in Palestine."

Eventually, eleven storage caves were found, yielding documentary fragments that, when pieced together, totaled about six hundred manuscripts, all dating from before the time of Christ.

We now know that a group of devoted Jews, probably Essenes, left the urban life of Jerusalem around 140 B.C. to settle in the hills of Judea. They founded the community of Qumran. During the Jewish rebellion of A.D. 66-72, Vespasian's legions decimated northern Israel and laid siege to Jerusalem. Around A.D. 68, as the Romans approached the Dead Sea area, the Qumran community placed their scrolls in storage in the nearby caves.

The arid climate preserved those documents so well that today we have a trove of Scripture predating our ninth-century documents by a thousand years.

How do those documents compare?

Two of the best-preserved documents are scrolls of the book of Isaiah. After examining them, Gleason Archer reported that these "proved to be word for word identical with our standard Hebrew Bible in more than 95% of the text. The 5% variation consisted chiefly of obvious slips of the pen and variations of spelling."[4]

Estimates like that are helpful to me, but specifics make it even clearer. The following is an example of the kind of accuracy discovered:

> Of the 166 words in Isaiah 53, there are only seventeen letters [in the Qumran scroll that differ from the standard Masoretic Text]. Ten of those letters are simply a matter of spelling, which does not affect the [meaning]. Four more letters are minor stylistic changes, such as conjunctions. The remaining three letters comprise the word "light," which is added in verse 11, and does not affect the meaning greatly.[5]

A GREAT QUESTION

In the movie *Multiplicity* Michael Keaton plays a building contractor who never has enough time for himself. Through advanced technology he clones himself. Soon his clone doesn't have enough time either. So the clone clones himself. What results is a clone of a clone that's slightly off. After all, everyone knows that every time you copy something, you lose a little quality.

Without studying the facts, it would seem reasonable to assume that the text of the Bible has degraded over the years. It's been 3,500 years since Moses wrote the Torah, and 2,000 years since John wrote the Revelation. How could the text *not* have diminished over time?

Then we check the records. With surprising detail, the text of Scripture seems to have been incredibly well preserved for all these years. In fact, the text has been so well preserved that Bible scholars conclude that God was not only involved in writing the original books of the Bible but has had his hand in their preservation as well. This is called the doctrine of divine superintendency.

We believe the transmission of God's words from one manuscript to the next has been divinely superintended or "watched over" so that what God wanted to say to every generation has been accurately conveyed to every generation from Moses to the present.

ASSIGNMENT
Read Deuteronomy 32:44-47.

1. These are some of the final words of Moses. What do they say about how important God's Word ought to be in your life?

2. What promises does Moses make to those who "obey carefully all the words of this law"?

5

Did God Really Write the Bible?

I must confess to you that the majesty of the scriptures astounds me. . . .
If it had been the invention of man, the invention would have
been greater than the greatest heroes.

Jean-Jacques Rousseau

◆　◆　◆

Across the centuries and cultures, people have believed that the
Bible is the Word of God. Does that mean that God wrote it? After
all, in chapter one I listed the authors of each book of the Bible. So
in what way did God participate in the writing of Scripture? In a
scientific culture like ours, it's hard to imagine a supernatural
presence breaking into the corporeal world. Yet most cultures in
history have had no problem with that idea.

Remember the Motilone tribesmen mentioned in chapter two?
This Stone Age culture had within its collective consciousness a
conviction that God had produced a means of communicating with
them. Being a preliterate society, the Motilones had no concept of a
book. They imagined God speaking through a banana stalk.

OTHER PEOPLES OF THE BOOK
Halfway around the world from the Motilones live the Lahu

people. The Lahu live on a tiny strip of Myanmar that borders China, Thailand and Laos. For centuries these people believed that Gui'Sha, the Creator of all things, had given their forefathers his law written on rice cakes!

According to legend their forefathers had eaten the rice cakes during a famine, rationalizing that now they would have God's word inside of them. The Lahu believed they could not fully obey Gui'Sha's laws until they regained the precise written form of his laws. Their holy men taught that when the right time came, Gui'Sha would send a white brother with a white book containing the laws of Gui'Sha.

Bordering the Lahu is a people called the Wa. The Wa were headhunters who believed that one day a white brother would come with a copy of the book they had lost. In the late 1800s, a prophet named Pu Chan began teaching that the Wa needed to cease headhunting because the time the white brother would come was fast approaching, and he might not share God's law if he saw them engaging in such practices.

In 1892, William Marcus Young brought his family to Myanmar (then known as Burma). He felt called by God to do mission work in this country. Settling in the city of Kengtung, a modern city by 1890s standards, Young began to preach from the Bible in the marketplace.

One day a group of men in tribal clothing surrounded Young as he preached. As they stared at his Bible they began pleading with him to follow them up to the mountains. "We have been waiting for you!" they explained. After some discussion, Young followed them. The Lahu people began responding to his message in droves. They had no trouble believing that God had written a book to them.

Meanwhile, Pu Chan, the prophet of the Wa people continued to teach that the white man with the book would come to them soon. One day he saddled a little pony and told his disciples to follow it to *a white brother bearing the book of Siyeh, the True God.*

The story gets a little crazy at this point, but it's documented by Don Richardson in *Eternity in Their Hearts*.[1] Pu Chan's pony traveled two hundred miles across mountain trails to the city of Kengtung. The beast turned into Young's missionary compound and stopped at an unfinished well. The Wa men who had been following it didn't understand what had happened—until they looked into the well and noticed a white man looking back up at them. "Hello strangers!" he said. "May I help you?"

The Wa messengers asked, "Have you brought the book of God?" Young nodded.

As you can imagine, this tribe of 100,000 people were very responsive to the man with the book. Embedded in their culture was the assurance that God had developed a means to communicate with them. The Bible claims to be that source.

INSPIRATION OF SCRIPTURE

All Scripture is God-breathed. The apostle Paul pointed us toward an understanding of God's influence on the Bible when he wrote, "All Scripture is God-breathed" (2 Timothy 3:16). There are three important words in Paul's statement. The first is the word *all*. Whatever influence God exerted on Scripture, he exerted it on *all* the words of the Bible. The second important word is *Scripture*. In the previous chapter we learned the five distinguishing marks that help us recognize what is Scripture and what isn't. The third and most important term is *God-breathed*. In Greek the word is *theopneustos*. It's a compound word (*theo* = God; *pnuestos* = breathed). *Theopneustos* literally means "breathed into by God."

Paul is saying that God breathed his thoughts, desires and content into the minds of the authors as they wrote each word of the sixty-six books of the Bible. Theologians describe this as *plenary* (all), *verbal* (words) and *inerrancy* (without error). As they wrote the original texts of Scripture, God breathed into the authors the words, concepts and ideas he wanted written, in the *way* he wanted them written. Somehow he did this through the unique personalities of each writer without compromising their free will.

Moved by the Holy Spirit. The apostle Peter helps us understand the process of inspiration further. He says, "Above all, you must understand that no prophecy of Scripture came about by the prophet's own interpretation of things. For prophecy never had its origin in the human will, but prophets, though human, spoke from God as they were carried along by the Holy Spirit" (2 Peter 1:20-21). Peter experienced God's "breathing into" while writing two books of the Bible. His personal experience was that he was moved by God to write what God wanted written. The writing was God's idea and God's initiative, using Peter and others to record it for him.

If that's true, how do we account for the different styles used by each author? Isaiah wrote with confidence. Jeremiah wrote with sorrow. Daniel used strange descriptions. John used simple words. Luke employed technical language.

The answer is, God prepared authors—their heredity, their experiences and the time they lived in history—to be able to understand and express exactly what he wanted written. The Holy Spirit worked in unique and supernatural ways so that each biblical author's written words were "the words of God."

The Word of God. Paul seems to have understood this intuitively. In 1 Thessalonians 2:13, he wrote, "We also thank God continually because, when you received the word of God, which you heard from us, you accepted it not as a human word, but as it actually is, the word of God, which is indeed at work in you who believe." At certain times when Paul wrote or spoke, he had a clear sense that God was "breathing" into him, communicating "the word of God" to his people.

WAYS GOD COMMUNICATED

Handwriting. Twice in the Bible (Exodus 24:12 and Daniel 5:5) God physically wrote what he wanted to say. The rest of the time, he used prophets and apostles to write for him.

Dictation. The various biblical authors wrote 413 times "This is what the LORD says" (or "Thus saith the LORD," in the King James Version). Scripture writers recorded the phrase "God said" around 3,800 times. An example of this is in Jeremiah 26:1-2: "This word came from the LORD: 'This is what the LORD says: . . . Tell them everything I command you; do not omit a word.'" God's "breathing" was so emphatic that at least 3,800 times the Bible's authors felt as if he was dictating to them.

Supernatural influence. First Corinthians 2:13 says, "This is what we speak, not in words taught us by human wisdom but in words taught by the Spirit, explaining spiritual realities with Spirit-taught words." Some portion of God's influence included teaching and explaining spiritual truths.

EXACT WORDS ARE IMPORTANT

In the final chapter of the book of Revelation God makes it clear that the precise words of his book are important.

> I warn everyone who hears the words of the prophecy of this scroll: If anyone adds anything to them, God will add to that person the plagues described in this scroll. And if anyone takes words away from this scroll of prophecy, God will take away from that person any share in the tree of life and in the Holy City. (Revelation 22:18-19)

Charles Wesley wrote,

> The Bible must be the invention of either good men or angels, bad men or devils, or of God. Therefore: 1. It could not be the invention of good men or angels, for they neither would nor could make a book and tell lies all the time they were writing

it, saying, "Thus saith the Lord," when it was their own invention. 2. It could not be the invention of bad men or devils,
for they would not make a book which commands all duty,
forbids all sin, and condemns their souls to hell to all eternity.
3. Therefore, I draw this conclusion, that the Bible must be
given by divine inspiration.[2]

ASSIGNMENT
Read 2 Timothy 3:14–4:2.

1. Why was it important for Timothy to have confidence in the
   words of Scripture?

2. Why is it important for you to have confidence in the words of
   Scripture?

3. What difference does it make whether the Bible is *the words of
   men* or *the Word of God*?

PART TWO
Purpose Questions

I believe the Bible is the best gift
God ever gave to man.

Abraham Lincoln

6

Does the Bible Speak to People?

Within the covers of one single book, the Bible, are all the answers to all the problems that face us today—if only we would read and believe.

Ronald Reagan

♦ ♦ ♦

During the sixth century B.C., the Jewish nation was conquered by the Babylonians and dragged into captivity. Seventy years later a group of fifty thousand men, women and children returned to Israel and resettled the land. Eighty years after that a smaller group also returned, led by Ezra the scribe. Rebuilding was hard. The people worked diligently, taking little time for worship, celebration or biblical instruction.

One day Ezra built a tall wooden platform and summoned the people to hear God's Word. He read the Scriptures from daybreak until noon. Then his helpers divided the people into small groups, making sure everyone understood what had been read. By the end of the day people were weeping (see Nehemiah 8). The Word of God had a powerful effect on them.

THE BIBLE LIVING IN YOU
The Bible presents some impressive claims for itself. One is that it

actually speaks to people. Hebrews 4:12 describes three ways that the Bible does this. It says, "The word of God is alive and active. Sharper than any double-edged sword, it penetrates even to dividing soul and spirit, joints and marrow; it judges the thoughts and attitudes of the heart."

The first way God's Word communicates is by living inside of us, actively helping us become more like Jesus.

Soon after I got married, I was reading the book of James when I saw this verse: "My dear brothers and sisters, take note of this: Everyone should be quick to listen, slow to speak and slow to become angry" (James 1:19). As I read those words, the Holy Spirit whispered to me, "You are quick to speak and slow to listen. Work on listening better."

I wrote "LISTEN" on a three-by-five card and taped it to my car's dashboard. For the next six months that card stared at me as I drove home from work, reminding me of what the Lord and I were working on together. I would greet Lori determined to make the conversation more about her and less about me. To this day I am not the world's greatest listener, but with God's help I am much better than I once was. From one encounter with the book of James, the Word of God began actively living in me.

THE BIBLE DOING SURGERY ON YOU

The second way God's Word communicates is by doing spiritual surgery on us: Hebrews says, "Sharper than any double-edged sword, it penetrates even to dividing soul and spirit."

In Bible times, one of the most advanced weapons was a double-edged sword. Older swords were only sharpened on one edge. Double-edged swords cut both directions. The Bible, as God's sword, does its work on the spiritual level. It slices us in the subtlest of ways: between our soul and our spirit. A physical sword will cut flesh. God's Word works on our character, outlook and priorities. In some ways it's like a spiritual scalpel, reshaping the ugly, flabby or dysfunctional parts of our soul.

One of the biggest struggles of the twenty-first century is materialism. Two hundred years ago a farmer made just about everything he needed and rarely thought about wanting things beyond his grasp. Today we have thousands of tools, products and gadgets to choose from, and with a little help from modern advertising, we want them all!

Frankly, out-of-control materialism is ugly. The urge for more drives people into debt. It goads us to work more hours than is healthy for our families. It drives us to jealousy when friends procure the latest toy. When God looks down on these out-of-control behaviors, I suspect he wants to put a knife to it. How does he do this? He speaks to us through his Word. Verses like Luke 12:15 are waiting to whisper to us: "Watch out! Be on your guard against all kinds of greed; life does not consist in an abundance of possessions." Passages like Matthew 6:19-21 call to us:

> Do not store up for yourselves treasures on earth, where moths and vermin destroy, and where thieves break in and steal. But store up for yourselves treasures in heaven, where moths and vermin do not destroy, and where thieves do not break in and steal. For where your treasure is, there your heart will be also.

I've known people who have read these verses and made significant lifestyle changes.

THE BIBLE CONVICTING YOU

The third way God's Word communicates is by presiding over us like a jury rendering a verdict on the things we're doing wrong. Hebrews says, "It judges the thoughts and attitudes of the heart."

One day I opened my Bible to Luke 14. Luke describes a sabbath day on which Jesus was invited to the home of a Pharisee. As the Lord arrived, a group of religious leaders were waiting on the porch. Stationed in front of them was an invalid, a man with edema. Edema is a condition that causes parts of one's body to retain fluid, swelling the limbs, torso or both. Jesus saw immediately that this man needed healing.

Turning to the Pharisees, Jesus asked, "Is it lawful to heal on the Sabbath?" They thought it was not. Jesus pushed them. "If one of you has a child or an ox that falls into a well on the Sabbath day, will you not immediately pull it out?" (vv. 3, 5).

To the chagrin of the Pharisees, Jesus healed the man and sent him on his way.

Their lack of compassion set Jesus just enough on edge that he decided to give them a second lecture once they got indoors. He watched as everyone was vying for the best seats at the table. He told them, "When someone invites you to a wedding feast, do not take the place of honor, for a person more distinguished than you may have been invited" (v. 8).

As I was reading this, the Spirit of God whispered to me, "Hal, find yourself in this picture." I was caught off-guard by that. First I had to figure out who was in this picture. In the screen of my mind, I saw a man with edema, a group of Pharisees and Jesus.

My first thought was, *Well, I don't have edema.* My second thought was, *And I'm certainly not Jesus.* That left only one option. I was a Pharisee.

In that moment I was tried, judged and convicted. "You are a Pharisee," God said to me. "You think you know what's right and wrong according to God's standards. You tend to look down on people who don't know God's standards the way you do. And you like taking nice seats at meetings and parties."

God was right! In that minute I felt broken, like someone had stuck a sword in my heart. I didn't know what to do about my condition, so I started to pray that God would change me. That encounter with God's Word altered my perception of myself, my attitude toward people and ultimately motivated me to leave the safe career path I was on. I moved my family a thousand miles to plant New Song Community Church. Luke 14 literally "judged the thoughts and attitudes of my heart."

ILLUMINATION

How does the Bible do that? I've never read a John Grisham novel that made me want to change. I've read some self-help books that offered me suggestions, but none of them cut me to the quick like Luke 14.

I don't know *how* the Bible speaks to us. I only know that it does. The communication comes from the Spirit of God speaking through the Word of God. But I can't explain the mechanics of how it happens. If God has ever spoken to you through Scripture, you know what I'm talking about.

In the spirit of full disclosure I should tell you that there are many times when I read the Bible and I *don't* hear God's voice. Most of the time I don't hear because I'm not in the mood to listen. I rarely hear from God when I'm distracted or thinking about other things or hoping that I *won't* hear from him so I won't have to do anything. Funny thing, that. When I come *not* listening, I don't hear.

It's for this reason that I try to pray an inviting prayer every time I sit down to read God's Word. Psalm 119:18 says, "Open my eyes that I may see wonderful things in your law." That's a great prayer. Ephesians 1:18 says, "I pray that the eyes of your heart may be enlightened." That's another great prayer. Ephesians 1:17 says, "I keep asking that the God of our Lord Jesus Christ, the glorious Father, may give you the Spirit of wisdom and revelation, so that you may know him better." That may be the best prayer of all for inviting God to speak to us.

Sometimes when I read the Bible I get nothing out of the particular passage I'm reading, but in the back of my mind I know exactly why nothing is striking me. At those times, as I listen to God's gentle whisper, I hear him saying, "Hal, I don't want you to do anything with the passage you're currently reading because I've already given you an assignment you're not fulfilling. Before we move on to something new, I want you to take care of the thing I've already asked you to do."

God is always speaking through his Word. My job is to listen and respond.

ASSIGNMENT

This week, before reading Scripture, I encourage you to invite the Holy Spirit to speak to you from his Word. Then, while you're reading, ask yourself, *What is God saying to me here?* and, *What does God want me to do with what he's saying?* Jesus observed, "My sheep listen to my voice" (John 10:27). You'll find the more you listen and respond to what God says, the more he will speak to you. Pray, read and listen.

Read 1 Corinthians 2:10-16. If what you're reading seems confusing, try reading it from a simpler version. You can access versions like the New Living Translation or *The Message* online at www.biblegateway.com.

1. What is the Bible saying in this passage? (Write it down. Writing forces us to clarify our thoughts.)

2. What is God saying *to me* as I read this?

3. What does God want me to do with what he's saying right now?

7

What's the Bible's Purpose?

We account the Scriptures of God to be the most sublime philosophy.

Isaac Newton

♦ ♦ ♦

The apostle John said he wrote his Gospel "that you may be-lieve" (John 20:31). What you believe may be the most important thing about you.

John actually says a little more than that. He says he wrote his book "that you may believe . . . and that by believing you may have life." The reason believing is so important is because what we be-lieve determines how we live. If we believe that generosity is a good thing, or if we believe that we will benefit by being generous, then we'll be generous. If we believe we have to work for every-thing that comes our way, or that the world owes us more than we owe it, we're more likely to hold onto what we have and let others fend for themselves.

Everyone sees the world through filtered lenses. Some people look at the world suspiciously. Others, skeptically. Still others, op-timistically. Every human being has a different perception of re-ality because we have differing backgrounds, experiences and points of view.

The only being in the universe who possesses complete sight and accurate vision is God. God needs no lenses because he created reality and experiences it fully.

God wants us to see and understand the world through his eyes because he created us to live the best life possible, both here and in eternity.

There's still a bit more that John said about the purpose of his book. His full statement is, "These are written that you may believe that Jesus is the Messiah, the Son of God, and that by believing you may have life in his name" (John 20:31).

THE PURPOSE OF THE BIBLE

The purpose of the Bible is that you may believe precisely what God knows to be true: that Jesus is the Messiah (the "Anointed One"), who came to initiate a relationship between you and God. If you will respond to his invitation to relationship, you will have "life in his name." *Life in his name* is a way of saying, "life in relationship with Jesus as your Lord."

The Old Testament was written to record God's preparation for the coming of his Son. It points forward to the birth, life, death and resurrection of Jesus. The New Testament was written to record the life of Jesus and invite us to live *life in his name.*

THE PURPOSE OF THE OLD TESTAMENT

Galatians 3:24 says, "The law was our guardian until Christ came." "The law" refers to the Old Testament. The word *guardian* is *paidagōgos* in Greek. In the first-century culture the *paidagōgos* was a slave assigned to walk the child to school and help him with his manners and homework. In other words, the Old Testament records the development of people and their understanding to the point where Christ could be born into the world and received as the "Anointed One," the Savior of the world.

Once Christ came, everything changed. The living Word walked among us. His teachings and miracles were documented by John and the other three Gospels' writers "that you may believe." Once we believe, the rest of the New Testament is designed to teach us how to live in light of our new faith in and relationship to the Son of God.

THE PURPOSE OF SCRIPTURE

Second Timothy 3:16-17 says, "All Scripture is God-breathed and is useful for teaching, rebuking, correcting and training in righteousness, so that the servant of God may be thoroughly equipped for every good work." The word for *useful* is *ōphelimos*. It means "profitable, helpful, serviceable."

The entirety of Scripture is useful for four things. *Teaching, rebuking, correcting* and *training in righteousness*. The Bible's four-step process is to teach us how to believe, how to see things the way God sees them. Then, it rebukes us, exposing how we're thinking wrongly when we stray. While pointing out our error, it corrects our course and thinking. Finally, it trains us to live the way God intended.

Think of this as the Second Timothy Road. The Bible *teaches* what is right, saying, "This is the road." When we get off the road, it rebukes us, saying, "You're off the road." Next it corrects us, saying, "This is how to get back on the road." Then it trains us in righteousness by saying, "This is how to stay on the road."

The rest of the passage says, "so that the servant of God may be thoroughly equipped for every good work." That's the goal: that by reading Scripture and letting it read us, we will become a people who have everything we need to do the right thing in every situation.

PUTTING IT TOGETHER

The Old Testament walks us to school, where we learn that we need Christ. The Gospels show us Christ and invite us to experience *life in his name*. The Epistles show us the road Christ wants us to walk. And Revelation reveals what's coming and how we'll be united with Christ for eternity.

No wonder Psalm 119:105 says, "Your word is a lamp for my feet, a light on my path." The purpose of the Bible is to help you see God and his will and his world clearly; and then live like it, in light of eternity.

In Isaiah 55:10-11 God claims,

> As the rain and the snow
>   come down from heaven,
> and do not return to it
>   without watering the earth
> and making it bud and flourish,
>   so that it yields seed for the sower and bread for the eater,
> so is my word that goes out from my mouth:
>   It will not return to me empty,
> but will accomplish what I desire
>   and achieve the purpose for which I sent it.

The Bible has a purpose, which it will accomplish!

PEOPLE WHO WAITED FOR THE BOOK

In a report titled "An Account of an Embassy to the Kingdom of Ava in the Year 1795," Lieutenant Colonel Michael Symes recorded an encounter he had with the Karen (Kaw-rin) people.[1] While arbitrating a dispute between the British and the Burmese, Symes was surrounded by a group of Karen in the city of Rangoon. With wide eyes, one man asked, "Did the white brother bring the White Book?" One of the Karen explained that the supreme God, Y'wa, had given them a book, but they had lost it and were therefore unable to live the way Y'wa intended.

Embedded in the Karen traditions was the knowledge that the supreme God had written a book whose purpose was to teach them how to have a relationship with him. Sound familiar?

Symes's account sat in the British diplomatic archives for over fifty years, until George Boardman and Sarah Boardman arrived as missionaries, bringing "the White Book." By 1858 tens of thousands of Karen were baptized in the name of Jesus. During my doctoral studies, I had a classmate from Burma. She was working on an advanced degree in Christian leadership so she could return to her country to teach in the seminary there. Like rain, the Word of God is fulfilling its purpose all over the world!

ASSIGNMENT
Read John 20:19-31.

1. What caused Thomas to believe (vv. 26-27)?

2. How did Thomas's new way of seeing change the way he lived?

3. Do you believe that Jesus is the Messiah? If you do, are you living like it, or are there some behaviors you need to align with your beliefs?

8

Can the Bible Make Me
a Better Person?

The existence of the Bible, as a book for the people,
is the greatest benefit which the human race has ever experienced.
Every attempt to belittle it is a crime against humanity.

Immanuel Kant

♦   ♦   ♦

At eight years old, Josiah became king. His father, Amon, had done such a poor job of ruling that he'd been assassinated by his own advisers. Josiah's grandfather, Manasseh, had been an equally poor ruler. Amon and Manasseh led the people away from God and abandoned his temple. We learned earlier that the scrolls of the Old Testament were stored in the temple.

When young Josiah realized the condition of his kingdom, he commissioned his priests to repair and reopen the temple. In what might be a comical scene if it wasn't both tragic and true, Hilkiah the high priest went into the temple and found the sacred scrolls. Apparently, no one had thought of, taught or handled God's Word for over a generation.

The king's secretary reported, "Hilkiah the priest has given

me a book" (2 Kings 22:10). He started reading it to the king.
When Josiah heard the words of the Book of the Law, he tore
his robes.

> Go and inquire of the LORD for me and for the people and for
> all Judah about what is written in this book that has been
> found. Great is the LORD's anger that burns against us be-
> cause those who have gone before us have not obeyed the
> words of this book; they have not acted in accordance with
> all that is written there concerning us. (2 Kings 22:13)

The Bible's epitaph on Josiah reads, "Neither before nor after
Josiah was there a king like him who turned to the LORD as he
did—with all his heart and with all his soul and with all his
strength, in accordance with all the Law of Moses" (2 Kings 23:25).

SIGNIFICANT CHANGES

One way to answer the question, Can the Bible make me a better
person? is to conduct a personal experiment: Read the Bible and
watch how it influences you over time.

Another way is to look for changes in others who have read or
are reading the Bible. The truth of God's Word changed Josiah
dramatically. The first time he heard it, it prompted him to tear his
robes, which was an ancient sign of repentance and mourning.

Or look at the Wa people. I'll bet if we asked their neighbors if
the Bible can make people better, they'd all agree that the Wa were
much improved, having given up their headhunting.

Likewise the Motilones. Fifteen years after Bruce Olson translated "God's banana stalk" for them, this once headhunting tribe
set up medical clinics and were offering free medical help to the
peoples they had once hunted.

FRANCIS KAMAU

I have a friend who planted a church in Nairobi, Kenya, a few years ago. His name is Francis Kamau. His people call him "Bishop" because of the work he's done in getting churches started all over English-speaking Africa.

Nairobi is a big city (population three million). When Francis prayed about where to start his church, he decided to locate it in an area that was filled with bars and brothels. The Bishop knew that God's Word changes lives, so he waded into an area that needed the most changing.

I preached at Francis's church not long ago. One of the church members gave Lori and me a ride to our hotel afterward. "See this boulevard?" he said. "When the Bishop first started, there were prostitutes all along this street. Today, many of them are members of our church and have found better ways to make money."

Can the words of a book really change lives? No. But the *truth* inside the words can, when infused with the power of the Holy Spirit. That's the dynamic of the Bible. Its truth, brought to life by the Spirit, changes lives every day. Sometimes those changes are big, like inspiring someone to stop killing à la the Wa and Motilones. Sometimes those changes are small, like prompting a child to be kinder to her mother, or encouraging an employee to stop taking company supplies for personal use.

HOW THE BIBLE CHANGES PEOPLE

Paul's pattern in his letters is to open with theology and close with practical application. The book of Romans covers some significant theology in its first eleven chapters, but then it shifts to application in chapter twelve. Based on what Christ has done for us, Paul says, "Do not conform to the pattern of this world, but be transformed by the renewing of your mind" (Romans 12:2).

Transformation begins with the mind. What you think about and how you think about it shape your attitude and behaviors every minute of the day. Growing up, I was a competitive swimmer. I would spend several hours each day counting laps and calculating times. As a result, I'm still pretty good with numbers today. Since becoming a Christian, I have spent significant time reading, studying and thinking about the words of the Bible. As a result of that, most of my thoughts these days are about God's plans for this world and how he wants me to treat people.

THINKING GOD'S THOUGHTS

We've already established that the Bible conveys the thoughts of God recorded in the words of men. The great virtue of reading and studying the Bible is that doing so enables us to think God's thoughts after him. If you want to know what God thinks about how you should treat people, read Matthew 22:39. He tells us clearly, "Love your neighbor as yourself." Or memorize Philippians 2:4, "Let each of you look not only to his own interests, but also to the interests of others" (ESV).

The thing about this world is, it's not the way God intended it to be. One day it will be restored to an Edenlike condition. For now, sin reigns, and creation is under a curse. Listen to your parents fight and your mind will absorb an image of a manner of fighting that is probably not the way God intended. Watch a television show and you'll see people do things to one another that certainly aren't what God planned.

But when we read the Bible and we come across statements like "Whoever wants to become great among you must be your servant" (Matthew 20:26), and "Whoever wants to save their life will lose it, but whoever loses their life for me will find it" (Matthew 16:25). These perspectives resonate with our souls, but they're not resident in our world, unless we learn and model them.

Paul said the way to avoid being conformed to the pattern of this world is to be transformed by the renewing of our minds. Anyone who grew up playing with Transformers and Decepticons knows that when they are "transformed" from machines to robots, they stay that way until they are deliberately changed back. The verb tense Paul uses for "transform" is a tense that means "transform and keep transforming." Being transformed is a continuous action. That's why people who start reading the Bible never stop reading it. We need continuous input so we don't change back.

Our world keeps sending us messages and models of an inferior way to do things. God's Word shows us a better way. To keep improving in this better way, keep feeding your mind on Scripture so you don't slip back into your old ways and patterns.

The Bible doesn't identify the author of Psalm 119, but whoever he was, he observed something profound: "I have hidden your word in my heart / that I might not sin against you" (Psalm 119:11). The Scripture he absorbed was diminishing his tendency to sin. That's an argument for memorizing portions of Scripture. The more your brain has top-of-the-mind-awareness of God's view of things, the less your heart will want to do things that hurt you and other people.

WHY IT'S HARD TO READ THE BIBLE

Most of the significant battles we face take place inside our mind. We want to be a more productive person. That means we've got to decide to go to bed earlier. We want to get in better shape. That means we've got to decide to work out. We don't like our job. That means we've got to decide to either have a better attitude or look for a new place of employment. God knew this principle, so he wrote us a book to help us think better. Then he infused his Holy Spirit into the book so that we would have supernatural help in understanding and applying what he wrote.

Satan knows this, which is part of the reason why it's hard to sit down and read the Bible. The deceiver of our souls will do almost anything to keep us from allowing our mind to be transformed. Ephesians 6:12 says, "Our struggle is not against flesh and blood, but against . . . the spiritual forces of evil." The struggle starts with our mind. Thankfully, the more we absorb Scripture into our mind, the easier it becomes not only to spend time reading the Bible but also to live like Jesus. Because belief determines behavior, and right behavior reinforces right belief.

Another reason we find it hard to read Scripture is because of what the Bible calls our "flesh." We're creatures of habit who don't like to change. Reading Scripture really will change us, and *we* know it intuitively. So every time our conscious mind says, *I want to read the Bible*, our subconscious mind retorts, *If you do, it will change you, and change is painful.*

The next time that happens, redirect the reasoning in your mind with this thought: *This kind of change will make my life better, because I'll become more of the person God intended me to be.* Then dig in and be transformed!

THE BIBLE AND CHILDREN

In Daniel 1, Daniel and his three best friends are enlisted by the Babylonian high court to take part in a counselor-in-training program. Besides being schooled in the classic learnings of the day, like history, geography and astronomy, they're pressured to conform to the pattern of the Babylonians by eating foods forbidden in the law of Moses.

With grace and aplomb, these four teenagers emerge three years later as the best of the best in their class. In every matter of wisdom and understanding, King Nebuchadnezzar himself accounts them ten times better than all the magicians and enchanters in his whole kingdom. How did this happen?

The one factor that was different for the four Hebrews than for all the other courtiers was their background in the Bible. Prior to coming to the palace Daniel and friends had studied the Scriptures at home, with their parents and countrymen. The Scriptures had transformed them in ways the court's tutors could not.

A similar thing happened to Timothy in the New Testament. One reason he was such an able leader was because of the transforming work the Bible had performed on him while he was growing up. Paul writes, "As for you, continue in what you have learned and have become convinced of, because you know those from whom you learned it, and how from infancy you have known the Holy Scriptures, which are able to make you wise for salvation through faith in Christ Jesus" (2 Timothy 3:14-15).

Can the Bible make you a better person? That's its purpose and promise. Read it and it will change your mind. As your mind changes, so will your behavior. It won't happen overnight. Like an athlete who goes to the gym every day, your transformation will take place little by little, over time. That's the secret to a whole new you!

ASSIGNMENT
Read Romans 12:1-3, 9-21.

1. How are the principles in vv. 9-21 different than the pattern of this world?

2. Which of these patterns do you need to change today, and how will you do it?

3. What sorts of Bible-absorption habits do you need to develop in order to continually transform your mind? Do you need to establish a habit of daily Bible reading? (If so, when and where will you do it?) Do you need to join a Bible study or small group? Would you like to start memorizing Scripture?[1]

9

What's the Central Message of the Bible?

There is a book that is worth all the other books in the world.

Patrick Henry

♦ ♦ ♦

Luke stands out among the Bible's authors in that he is the only Gentile writer of Scripture. As a trained physician, Luke carefully researched Jesus' life and then wrote an "orderly account" for us (Luke 1:3).

The largest portion of Luke's Gospel is the story of Jesus' final journey to Jerusalem. In Luke 9:51 Jesus "resolutely set out for Jerusalem." In Luke 19:28-44, Jesus made his triumphal entry into the holy city. For that reason, Luke 9–19 is sometimes called "Luke's travel narrative." Jesus starts in the north and walks south to Jerusalem. Each step brings him closer to his death on Passover for the sin of the world. Every word he utters on this journey is important. This is his last chance to communicate what really matters to him.

LUKE 15

In Luke 15, in the middle of this travel narrative, Jesus turns to the

Pharisees and gives them what may be the most important lecture in the Bible. Jesus was spending time with people considered beneath the dignity of a rabbi. He was rubbing shoulders with the "tax collectors and sinners." This offended the sensibilities of the Pharisees. They didn't like it. Behind his back there were muttering, "This man welcomes sinners and eats with them" (v. 2).

In response, Jesus told three parables back-to-back. In Matthew 13, Jesus tells five parables, explaining each one as he goes. In Luke 15, Jesus tells three parables with no explanation between them. It's the only time this happens in Scripture. It's as if Jesus is saying, "I'm going to tell you not one, not two, but three stories back-to-back so you will never again wonder why I came and what I'm all about."

The three parables of Luke 15 are the lost sheep, the lost coin and the lost son. The parable of the lost sheep begins with "Suppose one of you . . ." The story is designed to elicit a response. We might say it this way: "What would you do if . . ." In this case, Jesus is asking, "What would you do if you had a hundred sheep and lost one?" The parable of the lost coin starts the same way.

"Suppose a woman has ten silver coins and loses one?"

It's a good question. What do we do when we lose something of value? We look for it! Both the shepherd and the woman launch an all-out search to find what they've lost. When they find it, they are so happy they throw parties.

The third parable does not begin with "Suppose . . ." but with an objective statement: "There was a father who had two sons." This story isn't hypothetical. To Jesus, it is a very real analogy for what has happened in the heavenlies.

THE PRODIGAL FATHER

In this third parable Jesus outlines the central message of the Bible. It's typically called the parable of the prodigal son. I think we've mislabeled it. This is not a story of a son; it's the story of a father.

Dictionaries define *prodigal* as "recklessly wasteful" or "extravagant." The story Jesus told to the Pharisees on his way to Jerusalem is the story of a recklessly wasteful or extravagant father.

The story opens with a son saying, "Father, give me my share of the estate" (v. 12). To the Middle Eastern ear this was the same as saying "Father, I wish you were dead." Anyone hearing this request would immediately assume that the father would beat his son for such insolence. To their shock, the father doesn't retaliate. He complies with his son's wish by dividing his property between the two sons.[1]

What does the younger son do with his newly acquired wealth? A modern Westerner imagines him opening a checking account and applying for a debit card. Ancient Eastern listeners knew it wasn't that easy. People didn't keep their wealth in stocks and bonds, they kept them in land and cattle. When the father divided his wealth, he divided up his material possessions.

A second misperception we have in the West is that "my business is my business." Easterners believe that the actions of one member of the village reflect on all the members of the village. When the younger son wished his father dead, he not only insulted his father, he brought shame on every member of the village.

Imagine the scene: wherever the son goes, he is ostracized. He's hated in the village. He can't stay there. But in order to leave, he's got to liquidate his assets. Who will he sell them to? His only choice is to peddle his goods to the very villagers who are talking about tarring and feathering him.

Day by day he goes door to door, pawning his father's wealth. By the time he has sold everything, the village is seething. There's talk of a beating. The son has no choice; he *must* move away. Gathering together all that he has, the son sets off for a distant country.

Bear in mind that no matter how far he moved, the "distant country" would still be an Eastern country—with the same values of respecting one's elders and not bringing shame on one's village.

This ungrateful son burns through his inheritance like a torch through paper. Once his money is gone, he has no choice but to get a job.

How do the people of the distant country feel about this disrespectful son? Now that he has no money, they don't want him in their villages either. They've watched him waste his father's inheritance and want nothing to do with him.

Nevertheless, hospitality is highly valued in the Middle East. They can't out and out refuse this young man's request for a job. Instead, they offer him one they know he can't accept. This Jewish boy is offered a job feeding pigs. Pigs are ritually unclean to the Jews. And pigs have to be fed seven days a week. Jews are forbidden to work on the sabbath. The villagers in the distant land offer the young man a job he cannot take. Yet he does. He agrees to feed pigs.

In Jesus' masterful telling, while feeding pigs, this wayward son comes to his senses:

> How many of my father's hired servants have food to spare, and here I am starving to death! I will set out and go back to my father and say to him: Father, I have sinned against heaven and against you. I am no longer worthy to be called your son; make me like one of your hired servants. (vv. 17-19)

It's a three-part speech. Part one is a confession. I have sinned against heaven and against you. Part two is a type of repentance. I am no longer worthy to be called your son. Part three is a request. Make me like one of your hired servants. The son rehearses this speech repeatedly during his long walk home.

Pause for a minute and imagine you are this younger son. You know how the villagers feel about you. You know that your father lives in the middle of the village, and village life is a communal life. The more important you are to the community, the closer you live to the center of town. You know that as soon as one of the villagers spots you, word will spread and there is a good chance you'll be met with jeers, probably swearing, and quite possibly rods and rocks. Yet you must make it to your father, because he is your only hope.

This is the mindset of the younger son as he makes his way into the village. Just as he has feared, word spreads quickly: "The pariah is back!" He closes his eyes, expecting stones and spittle.

Jesus now focuses our attention on the father. "But while he was still a long way off, his father saw him and was filled with compassion for him; he ran to his son, threw his arms around him and kissed him" (v. 20).

Instead of stones, the son feels loving arms wrapped around him. Instead of spittle, he receives kisses. Literally, Jesus said, "Running, he fell on his son's neck and kissed him repeatedly."

The son begins his well-rehearsed speech: "Father, I have sinned against heaven and against you. I am no longer worthy to be called your son." That's as far as he gets. The third part of his speech is missing. During this last portion of the speech, the son imagined himself falling at his father's feet and saying, "Make me like one of your hired servants." But he can't say it. Why? Because the father won't let him. The father has wrapped his arms around his son's neck so tightly he cannot fall to the ground. And the kisses are coming so rapidly that the whole idea is impossible. How could a son ask such a loving father to let him become a hireling?

The next words the son hears are these, "Quick! Bring the best robe and put it on him. Put a ring on his finger and sandals on his feet. Bring the fattened calf and kill it. Let's have a feast and celebrate. For this son of mine was dead and is alive again; he was lost and is found."

A Western ear might hear a father barking orders to his servants. An Eastern ear hears this as a soliloquy of grace. Every command the father gives is designed to make a point. The *best robe* is to be put on the son's back. Who owns the best robe? The father. A ring is to be put on his finger. This would be the family signet ring. The ring that sealed all legal documents. The son is given a ring which grants him power to do business in the name of his father. Sandals are to be brought because slaves go barefoot, but sons wear sandals. This is nothing less than the full restoration of the son to the family!

The servants are to kill *the fattened calf.* Why not the fattened chicken? Or the fattened goat? In societies without refrigeration, a family only prepared as much meat as they intended to eat that day. The rest would spoil. If the family was sitting down by themselves, they might consume a chicken's worth of meat. If they invited the extended family, a goat would suffice. To kill the largest animal meant you wanted to celebrate with everyone you knew! That's the command the father issues—he insists that the entire village celebrate his joy and reconcile with his returning son.

THE CENTRAL MESSAGE

This is a story no one could anticipate. A father who is so recklessly extravagant with his love that when the son wishes him dead, he extends grace. When the son approaches to earn his way back into the family, he is granted the full rights of sonship. His restoration is based on nothing he has done or can do, only on the outrageous love of the father.

This is the central message of the Bible: the heavenly Father is a "compassionate and gracious God, slow to anger, abounding in love and faithfulness, maintaining love to thousands, and forgiving wickedness, rebellion and sin" (Exodus 34:6-7).

The apostle Paul summarizes the central message in one sentence: "The wages of sin is death, but the gift of God is eternal life in Christ Jesus our Lord" (Romans 6:23). The apostle John summarizes: "God so loved the world that he gave his one and only Son, that whoever believes in him shall not perish but have eternal life" (John 3:16). Luke completes the thought with the father's pronouncement: "'For this son of mine was dead and is alive again; he was lost and is found.' So they began to celebrate" (Luke 15:24).

Preachers often end their sermons there, but the story is only half told. This is the story of a father who had *two* sons.

THE OLDER BROTHER

Middle Easterners always tell their stories according to a *chiastic* pattern. *Chi* is the Greek letter that looks like our letter X. If you shave off the right side of the X, you have a *chiasm*.

The story of the younger son is a perfect chiasm. The story begins with a son who is lost. Call this A. It ends with a son being found. This is *A prime* (A'). The son leaves and wastes his money (B). When the son returns, his father wastes money (B'). The story progresses like this toward the climax in the center, which is the son's change of mind. He "came to his senses." The chiasm looks like this:

A   A son is lost
   B   Goods wasted in wild living
      C   Everything lost
         D   The Great Sin (feeding pigs for Gentiles)
            E   Total rejection
               F   Change of mind
            E'   Total acceptance
         D'   The Great Repentance ("I am unworthy")
      C'   Everything gained
   B'   Goods wasted in wild partying
A'   A son is found[2]

The story has perfect symmetry. There are variations of this structure, but Middle Easterners are so used to this storytelling pattern, it's instinctual with them. They listen for this pattern like we listen for the notes on the octave scale.

The second half of Jesus' parable is about the older son. This scene opens with the older brother conspicuously absent from the party.

The older son has distanced himself from the father as well. You can see it in his introduction: "Meanwhile, the older son was in the field" (v. 25). The field was outside the village. When the older brother heard how his sibling had been treated, "Your father has killed the fattened calf because he has him back safe and sound," he refused to join the party.

In Middle Eastern families, the older son serves as the host for all parties. This son balks at playing his role. Once again, the father approaches his son. This time, the father extends his arms to a son who has not moved away physically but relationally. You can see it when the son says, "You never gave me even a young goat so I could celebrate with my friends" (v. 29). Notice that the older son doesn't consider his father's friends to be *his* friends. Father and son travel in separate circles.

Back at the house, every guest would expect to be greeted by the older as they came to the front door. But the son isn't there. Once again, the village knows that a son is insulting his father.

The father's appeal includes an explanation that had never dawned on the older son: when the father divided his estate, the younger son received his portion and so did the older son. "Everything I have is yours," says the father (v. 31).

Jesus ends the parable like this: "My son," the father said, "you are always with me, and everything I have is yours. But we had to celebrate and be glad, because this brother of yours was dead and is alive again; he was lost and is found" (v. 32).

The story of the older son is also a chiasm. Only this chiasm is incomplete.

A   A son is far off
   B   "Your brother is safe"—a feast
      C   Father comes to reconcile
         D   "How you treated me"
         D' "How you treated him"
      C' Father tries to reconcile
   B' "Your brother is safe"—a feast[3]

The conclusion is missing. Instead of resolving, this parable ends like a song on a dissonant note. An Easterner, used to hearing stories in this pattern, would ask, "But how does it end?"

The answer is, *There is no ending.* Jesus' story doesn't finish, it stops. This is a technique used by master storytellers to provoke a visceral response in their listeners. It forces the listener to generate his or her own conclusion. "How does the story end? Does the older son come home, or does he stay out in the field?" The listener must complete the story, using his or her own response as the answer.

What Jesus is saying to the Pharisees, and to all who will listen, is, "Son, will you come inside? All that I have is yours. Will you come home?"

This is the central question of the Bible.

Will you come home?

ASSIGNMENT
Read Luke 15.

1. What do the three parables have in common?

2. How do you respond to a God who is willing to put his robe on your back, his ring on your finger, his sandals on your feet and kill the fattened calf to celebrate your return?

3. Have you come home to the Father? If not, why not do so now by praying this prayer:

   Lord Jesus, I am coming home to you now. I admit that I have wandered away from you. I have done things that have caused you shame and am no longer worthy to be called your son/daughter. But because you invite me, I come. From today forward, be my Lord and Savior.

4. You may have prayed a prayer like this at some time in the past, but are you fully home or still out in the field? Do you need to

pray, admitting some way in which you've distanced yourself from the Father? If so, consider praying this prayer now:

Lord, here is an area I've been keeping away from you: _____. I give it to you now and ask you to take the role as my Father again. I want to honor you as a son/daughter and not shame you anymore.

5. Thank God for his reckless love for you.

10

What's the Bible's Story Line?

*The Bible has been the book that held together
the fabric of Western civilization. . . . The civilization we possess
could not come into existence and could not
have been sustained without it.*

H. G. Wells

♦ ♦ ♦

One of the most impressive characteristics of the Bible is its
cohesiveness. This book, which was coauthored by forty people
from different backgrounds and professions, with different languages and cultures, has one story line that runs from Genesis
to Revelation.

THE GOD WHO IS IN COMMUNITY

The story of the Bible is the story of God. The theme that runs
through all 1,189 chapters is that God is building a community of
people who relate to him by faith and one another in love so that
he can bless them, and through them, bless the world.

We can see this from the very first verse. Genesis 1:1 begins
with "In the beginning God created the heavens and the earth."
The Hebrew word for God here is *Elohim*. When we want to make

a word plural in English, we add an s to the end. In Hebrew, *im* is added. Eloh*im* is plural. It's a hint at God's nature. Some call this "the plural of majesty." Kings often refer to themselves in the plural, not the singular. Why shouldn't God do the same?

In Genesis 1:2 we find that "the Spirit of God was hovering over the waters." In Genesis 1:3, God said, "Let there be light." John explains that "in the beginning was the Word, and the Word was with God, and the Word was God" (John 1:1). The Word was Jesus. When God the Father *spoke* the world into existence, he did so through the agency of his Son, the Word. Therefore, Jesus is sometimes called the intermediate agent of creation.

God the Father created everything through God the Son, and God the Spirit was hovering over the waters. In the first three verses of the Bible, we find the Father, the Son and the Holy Spirit. God himself is a community, Three in One. This God, who has always enjoyed triune fellowship, wanted to share that fellowship with others.

Why did God decide to create the universe when he did? Genesis 1:2 says that "the earth was formless and empty." We don't actually know. Some speculate that the earth was formless at that time because of a war that had taken place between the angels of God and the fallen angels of Lucifer. This is called "the gap theory." A battle took place that left the earth formless and void. The battle also saw the defection of a significant number of angels. Hence, the size of God's community was diminished.

BUILDING COMMUNITY

If this is the case, God may have been prompted to create the physical universe out of a desire to extend community to a new species of free willed, sentient beings. In any case, the triune God created the universe to extend fellowship. By the end of his six days of creative work, the earth was populated with plants, fish, birds and animals, and Adam was installed as ruler and caretaker of the world. God looked on his work and pronounced it *very good* (v. 31).

In Genesis 2, God created Eve. Community was extended to a second gender of humans. Adam and Eve had such a close relationship with God that he walked with them in the Garden (Genesis 3:8) on a regular basis.

THE LOSS OF COMMUNITY

Genesis 3 opens with a serpent tempting Eve. Having rallied a portion of the angels to his side, Satan now seeks to further enhance his reputation and diminish God's glory by enlisting the humans among his followers. Adam and Eve eat the fruit of the tree of the knowledge of good and evil, the one action forbidden by God. A curse descends on all of creation.

Adam and Eve feel shame for the first time. God, in his mercy, begins his reconciling work. He offers hope by predicting that one day the offspring of a woman will crush the head of the serpent (Genesis 3:15). He then clothes the humans with animal skins. Where did this sacrifice come from? We don't know but the most likely answer would be from animals sacrificed on behalf of Adam and Eve. If that's the case, then this is the first of many foreshadowings of God's ultimate act: to reconcile human kind to himself through the death of an innocent creature.

In a sense Genesis 3 is the hinge point of the Bible. Genesis 1–2 is the story of paradise created. Genesis 3 is the story of paradise lost. Genesis 4 onward is the story of paradise regained.

Paradise is both a place and a condition. Our first parents not only lost the beauty and perfection of the Garden, they lost the intimacy and companionship of God.

All great stories use tension to hold the attention of their audience. The greater the tension, the more gripping the story. The Bible's tension comes from humanity losing their place in paradise and their relationship with God. How will they get that back?

That's the story of the Bible: the story of God rebuilding community with people who have lost their way. We see it in Luke 15.

We also see it in real life. The Motilone people long to have God's banana stalk reveal how to get right with God again. The Karen, Lahu and Wa peoples wait for a man with a book to tell them how to get back to the good graces of the one true God.

REBUILDING COMMUNITY

In Genesis 4 the rebuilding begins. God knows that we will make mistakes in our efforts to finding our way back to him. He decides to demonstrate the futility of those efforts by showing us, upfront, that they won't work. Genesis 4–11 is the story of three flawed solutions for finding our way back to God.

False starts. The first of these solutions is what I call, the "isolation solution." Out of jealousy, Cain kills his brother, Abel. God isolates Cain from the rest of humanity so he can't hurt or be hurt by others.

Isolation is the Buddhist solution for finding God. Buddhists believe the chief reason we feel pain and suffering is because we have *cravings*. We want things we don't have. If we didn't want things or care about people, we wouldn't experience feelings of loss or disappointment. The Buddha taught that the key to a peace-filled life is to eliminate cravings. If you don't care, you can't get hurt.

The isolation solution doesn't work. When Cain hears that he must spend his life outside of the community, he cries out, "My punishment is more than I can bear" (Genesis 4:13).

Genesis 6–9 presents the "repetition solution." As humanity expands, so does its profanity: "The LORD saw how great the wickedness of the human race had become on the earth" (Genesis 6:5). So God invites Noah to build an ark and start humanity over after the great flood (Genesis 7:1-4).

Some people believe that if they can just have a second chance at life, things will turn out better. The Hindu religion teaches that given enough lifetimes people can work their way to perfection. Through the flood account God shows that this solution won't work. Noah was "a righteous man, blameless among the people of his time, and he walked faithfully with God" (Genesis 6:9). Yet, within days of exiting the ark, Noah gets drunk, falls asleep naked and curses one of his own sons when the son mocks his nakedness (Genesis 9:20-25). The second chance doesn't work. Humanity is right back where it started, no closer to God.

The third option people often choose for finding their way back to God is the "exertion solution." In Genesis 11, people have settled on the plains of Mesopotamia. They decide to build a tower to reach heaven. It's their attempt to work their way back to God.

Exertion is the Muslim solution to loss of community. Muhammad taught that by diligently working the Five Pillars of Islam, a Muslim can earn Allah's favor and a place in paradise. Mormons, Jehovah's Witnesses and other religions also practice this work-related method of getting to God.

God knows that building a tower won't rebuild community, so he confuses the peoples' languages, causing them to abandon their effort-based solution for getting to God.

Community begins. Once the Lord has demonstrated the futility of these three approaches, he begins his community-rebuilding process in Genesis 12.

God chooses one man, Abraham, and begins to build a relationship with him. He promises,

> I will make you into a great nation
>> and I will bless you;
> I will make your name great,
>> and you will be a blessing. . . .
> [A]nd all peoples on earth
>> will be blessed through you. (Genesis 12:3)

God's one stipulation is that Abraham must trust him. Genesis 15:6 says, "Abram believed the LORD, and he credited it to him as righteousness."

God's plan is to initiate a relationship with one man, and through him to extend community to as many as possible. His goal is to build a community of people who relate to him by faith, and to one another in love so he can bless them, and through them, bless the world.[1]

God is by nature a blessing God. He loves to bless people. He knows that people who hoard blessings ultimately diminish that blessing, so his desire is to bless us so that we in turn will bless others. This is God's way.

Community extended. The rest of the book of Genesis is the story of how community is extended. Abraham in his old age miraculously fathers a son named Isaac, and the community expands. Isaac fathers a son named Jacob, and the community expands some more. Jacob has twelve sons, and the community expansion accelerates.

By the opening of the book of Exodus, the community that started with Abraham has become a nation of two million people. The community is so large it's a threat to Pharaoh. He enslaves the sons of Jacob until they cry out to God. When that happens, God sends them a deliverer named Moses.[2]

Moses is the great liberator of the community. He invokes ten plagues that demonstrate God's superiority over the gods of Egypt. The final plague is the judgment of the firstborn. The Lord promises that each Israelite family will be spared from this judgment provided they sacrifice a lamb and sprinkle its blood on the doorposts and lintels of their houses (Exodus 12:7). God asks them to do this annually. For the next fourteen hundred years the community expresses faith by sacrificing a Passover lamb as a substitutionary payment for their sins.

Pharaoh lets God's people go. They camp at Mount Sinai, where God gives them his law. The law teaches them how to love one another and relate to God by faith.

In the book of Leviticus, God teaches them how to worship him.

In order to have community, you need both a people and a place. The people are now relating to God by faith. The next step is the place.

In Numbers and Deuteronomy God prepares the people to enter the Promised Land. Joshua records the conquest of the Promised Land. Judges through Esther describe the struggles God's people have as they attempt to live by faith and relate to one another in love. During this period, prophets foretell that one day a son of David will sit on Israel's throne as the anointed one.

The books of poetry (Job through Song of Songs) provide wisdom for a life of faith. The books of prophecy (Isaiah through Malachi) record God's revelations to the people. Several prophets promise that one day the Lord will send a deliverer who will rescue the people from their sin once and for all. Isaiah predicts that an anointed one will be "led like a lamb to the slaughter," "pierced for our transgressions," and that "the punishment that brought us peace" will be upon him. (Isaiah 53:7, 5).

The final Old Testament prophet, Malachi, promises that one day "the sun of righteousness will rise with healing in its rays" (Malachi 4:2). This *sun of righteousness* will be preceded by one who will prepare a path for him.

The new community. The New Testament opens with Matthew tracing the lineage of Jesus Christ all the way back to Abraham. The genealogy includes David. From one generation to another God has been preparing his people for what is about to happen: the birth of the "sun of righteousness" who brings healing. Jesus' birth is announced by angels, witnessed by shepherds.

Up to this point in history, God's community largely has been made up of descendants of Abraham. Not long after Jesus' birth, wise men come "from the east" to worship the son of David. Their coming signals what is about to happen: God is about to open the community to Gentiles.

The four Gospels record the life of Jesus. They focus on the one event that is our ultimate solution for finding our way back to God.

It's the "substitution solution." On Passover A.D. 33 Jesus is led like a lamb to the slaughter. He's brought into Jerusalem through the Sheep's Gate, the exact gate through which Passover lambs had been herded for centuries on their way to be sacrificed at the temple.

Jesus, the "Lamb of God, who takes away the sin of the world" (John 1:29), is crucified on Calvary. With his final breath he announces, "It is finished" (John 19:30). What is finished? The story of God's rebuilding of community.

By offering his life in payment for our sin, Jesus, Lamb of God, the son of David, the righteous One, gives us a way to be reconciled to God. Instead of isolation, he offers community. Instead of endless repetition, he offers a one-time solution for our failures. Instead of exertion, he does the work for us. Our job is to accept God's invitation and enter into community with him through Jesus' sacrifice on our behalf on the cross.

Three days after Passover, Jesus rose from the dead on the Jewish holiday called "Firstfruits." What happened during the holiday week was foretold in the Jewish festivals. The Lamb was slain on Passover and the Firstfruits (of heaven) began three days later.

Jesus then trained his disciples to continue his work of building the community of faith. Jesus ascended to heaven. Fifty days after Passover, on Pentecost, which is the Jewish festival of harvest, the Holy Spirit descended and the harvest of people began, as the church was born.

The church is God's community of faith on earth. Once the fuse was lit on God's invitation to community, it spread like wildfire throughout the world. The book of Acts is the story of the church's rapid spread.

The Epistles were written to teach this rapidly spreading community how to relate to God by faith and to one another in love so that God can bless us, and through us bless the world.

The final book of the Bible describes the end of the world. After a cataclysmic war (Revelation 4–18), Christ will return to end that war and reign on the earth for one thousand years (Revelation 19–20). At the end of those thousand years, there will be a final judgment (Revelation 20:11-14), followed by a new heaven and a new earth (Revelation 21–22).

This is the story of the Bible. It opens with two chapters of paradise. Its third chapter records how paradise was lost and how judgment was pronounced on humanity. Its third-to-last chapter records how paradise will be regained, and how judgment will be pronounced on those who reject God's offer of community. The Bible closes with two chapters on the coming of the new paradise. The Bible story is presented as a chiasm.

God, who is in community with himself, created the world in order to expand community to people like us. The Bible is the story of God building a community of people who relate to him by faith and to one another in love so that he can bless us, and through us bless the world.

ASSIGNMENT

Read Acts 2:36-47.

1. What aspects of community do you see here?

2. What aspects of living by faith do you see here?

3. What aspects of relating to one another in love do you see here?

PART THREE

Probing Questions

It is the best book that ever was,
or ever will be written.

Charles Dickens

11

Why Are There So Many Translations?

Translation it is that openeth the window, to let in the light,
that breaketh the shell, that we may eat the kernel;
that putteth aside the curtain, that we may look into the most Holy place;
that removeth the cover of the well, that we may come by the water,
even as Jacob rolled away the stone from the mouth of the well,
by which means the flocks of Laban were watered.

Preface to the King James Version of the Bible (1611)

♦ ♦ ♦

One of Christianity's most sacred sites is the Church of the Nativity in Bethlehem. Toward the front of this church is a stone staircase leading down to the place where many believe Mary gave birth to Jesus. On the opposite side of the wall from there is a cave with evidence that suggests it housed the Holy Family until their escape to Egypt. Ten feet from this cave is a larger cavern where St. Jerome completed his translation of the Bible into Latin in A.D. 405. According to historians, Jerome wanted to be near the birthplace of his Lord while he completed this sacred task.

Jerome's Bible is called the Vulgate. It was the official Roman

Catholic version of the Bible for more than a thousand years. Conceivably, more people have been influenced by Jerome's translation of the Bible than by any other book in history.

THE SEPTUAGINT

In Jesus' day the most popular version of the Old Testament was a Greek translation called the Septuagint. By the time of Christ, Greek was the trade language throughout the Roman Empire. Most Jews used the Septuagint as their normal reading Bible. Naturally, the first Christians used this same Greek translation as their Old Testament Scriptures, just as English speakers use English translations today.

Since the New Testament was composed in Greek, very few early Gentile Christians felt the need to learn Hebrew. Their Bible was the Greek Bible. By the fourth century several people had translated the Greek Bible into Latin. Jerome's translation was unique in that he used the Hebrew text of the Old Testament to make his translation into Latin.

The Vulgate was clearly an improvement over the Greek-to-Latin versions. You'd expect the church to rejoice in Jerome's efforts. Yet, when Augustine of Hippo read Jerome's Vulgate, he felt the need to write a letter and object:

> My only reason for objecting to the public reading of your translation from the Hebrew in our churches was, lest bringing forward anything which was, as it were, new and opposed to the authority of the Septuagint version, we should trouble by serious cause of offense the flocks of Christ, whose ears and hearts have become accustomed to listen to that version to which the seal of approbation was given by the apostles themselves.[1]

Augustine didn't like Jerome's translation because its words were unfamiliar. His people had "become accustomed" to other words.

They preferred the *less accurate* to the *familiar.* Thus was born a debate that continues to our day.

1. When translating, what texts will we translate *from?*

2. What type of words will we translate *to?*

For professional translators, these are called *textual questions* and *translational questions.*

TEXTUAL QUESTIONS

Prior to Jerome, Latin versions were made from the Old Testament secondary language of Greek. That rarely happens today. Modern translators base their work on the primary languages. In our day, when a committee begins a new translation, their question is, What was the original text?

For the Old Testament these decisions are relatively simple. Because of the careful work of the Masoretes (see chap. 3), translators generally use the Masoretic text, with help from the Dead Sea Scrolls and a few other ancient manuscripts. Sometimes they will also consult ancient secondary translations (such as the Septuagint) for further comparison and accuracy.

With the New Testament, because of the abundance of manuscripts available, things are more complicated. Fortunately, an international committee of scholars, working together as the United Bible Society, has been keeping track of new textual developments for the past several decades. This committee has rated the reliability of *every word* of the New Testament. They update these ratings every few years, taking advantage of the newest textual discoveries.

Still, there are a few textual questions to wrestle with. To appreciate this, we have to know something about church history. As Christianity spread throughout the Roman Empire, centers of regional authority developed around the cities of Alexandria in Africa, Rome in the West, Constantinople in the East, and Antioch and Jerusalem in the Middle East. The bishops of these cities gave help and advice to the pastors of the churches in their areas.

If a pastor in Africa needed a new copy of the Bible, chances were good he would make that copy from one in Alexandria. If a pastor in Italy needed a Bible, he would copy one from Rome. If a scribe in one of those cities made an error in copying, that error would make its way into many subsequent copies. Most of those copies would remain within that region of churches.

For instance, if a copyist in Africa wrote "in" when he should have written "on," many copies within the African region would include that same error. Whereas the copies in the East, West and Middle East would still read "on." At the same time, a copyist in the East might write "eat" where he should have written "ate." Soon most Eastern copies would read "eat," while the other three regions of texts would carry the original "ate."

What scholars have discovered is that there are four distinct *families* of text types. Errors developed regionally.

In chapter four we learned that there is relatively little disagreement between the ancient texts. But, as you'd expect, the disagreements that do exist vary by region.

Three choices. When a committee comes to the "in" versus "on" variant, which one do they choose? Some believe in using *the majority text*. If there are ten thousand manuscripts and 80 percent read "in," then "in" becomes the choice.

Here's where it gets sticky. Because Constantinople became the seat of the Roman Empire and survived in relative peace for a thousand years, we have many more copies of that region's text than the other three regions combined.

A second way to settle the textual question is to follow the *oldest text*. The older the text, the less times it was probably copied, and therefore the lesser chance for errors to creep in. Most of the oldest manuscripts, including Sinaiticus and Alexandrinus, come out of the Alexandrian family.

A third method for word choice is to compare the four families. Do three of the four agree on a particular word or phrase? If so, it's likely that the three are correct, rather than the one.

TRANSLATIONAL QUESTIONS

The other important question is, How will we translate?

When I thank the store's cashier, she says, "You're welcome." I thank a Marine for serving our country and he responds, "No problem." I thanked a young person the other night, and he said, "No worries." There is always more than one way to say things in any language. Translators have to decide between three styles of translation.

Three styles. One style is called "formal equivalence." Formal equivalence tries to maintain a word-for-word translation from one language to another. The advantage of this is accuracy. The disadvantage is understandability. When I say thank you to my Spanish-speaking gardener, he responds, "De nada." A literal translation of that would be, "It was of nothing." We don't usually speak like that in English, but it works perfectly for Spanish speakers.

Greeks like to begin their sentences with the most important word. English speakers like to lead with the subject of the sentence. Formal equivalence translations strive for accuracy, sometimes at the expense of normal English grammar.

A second style is called "dynamic equivalence." This style concentrates on capturing the *meaning* from one language to the other. It's sometimes called an idea-for-idea translation. Its advantage is clarity. Its disadvantage is less precision. My gardener says "De nada." I translate that as "You're welcome" because that's how we say it in English, even though I know that a more accurate translation is, "It was of nothing."

In Greek, Luke 9:44 reads: *Thesthe hymeis eis ta hōta hymōn.*" A literal word-for-word translation of this would be "Lay you in the ears of you." Obviously, this doesn't sound quite right.

The English Standard Version, which is a formal equivalent translation, attempts to keep the accuracy of the statement by translating it as "Let these words sink into your ears."

The New International Version (NIV), a dynamic equivalent translation, tries to keep the clarity of what's being said by translating it as "Listen carefully to what I am about to tell you."

A third stylistic option is a paraphrase. Technically, a paraphrase isn't a translation, because it doesn't attempt to translate the Bible's words. Instead, a paraphrase tries to capture the Bible's concepts. *The Message,* which is a modern paraphrase, reads, "Treasure and ponder each of these next words."

All three of these options started with the same Greek words. Their translational choices led them to very different English words. The upside of a paraphrase is that its author can create word plays and phrases that spark new thinking in the reader's mind. For instance, where the NIV translates Romans 12:2 as "Do not conform to the pattern of this world," J. B. Phillips's translation renders it "Don't let the world around you squeeze you into its own mould."

The downside of paraphrases is they reflect the theological bents and bias of their author. I own three paraphrases, *The Message,* the Living Bible and the J. B. Phillips translation, and enjoy reading them from time to time. But I think of them more as commentaries than the definitive words of Scripture.

Before a person or team sits down to do their work, a set of rules is established to determine translational style and other parameters as well.

THE ANSWER

Why do we have so many translations? Because we live in a day when we have the luxury of extensive scholarship (utilizing textual choices) and a variety of purposes (choices of accuracy versus clarity of style).

One reason so many English versions have come on the market in recent years is because of the acceleration of information in our world. Over the past fifty years there's been an explosion of knowledge. The advance of archaeology has uncovered many new texts and fragments of texts. Advances in lexicology (the study of words) has aided in further understanding. The speed of communication has accelerated the change that takes place in language. All these make it necessary to revise dated translations and encourage the development of new versions and paraphrases.

POPULAR VERSIONS
In 2010 the five best-selling English Bibles were

1. New International Version

2. King James Version

3. New King James Version

4. New Living Translation

5. English Standard Version

New International Version. The NIV is a dynamic equivalent translation. Over one hundred biblical scholars were involved in this translation. A fifteen-member committee on Bible translation made the final editorial decisions and maintains vigilance over the text to this day. The committee's goal is an accurate, beautiful, clear and dignified translation. The NIV New Testament was released in 1973, the entire Bible in 1978. The committee on Bible translation makes minor revisions from time to time, with a major revision, NIV 2011, released in 2011.

King James Version family. The KJV was authorized by King James I of England and published in 1611. The KJV is a formal equivalent translation. The translators were some of the greatest minds ever assembled in the English-speaking world. Many believe that its lyrical English set the high watermark of English literature. The KJV (or "Authorized Version") was based largely on the Eastern family of texts, and therefore may not have utilized the best textual choices.

Improved scholarship has been applied to the Authorized Version (AV) in almost every generation. The AV, New American Standard Bible and several other versions are part of this family of translations.

In 1982, 130 Bible scholars completed a revision of the KJV that is called the New King James Version (NKJV). This version attempts to maintain the familiar style and language of the KJV while eliminating archaic language and applying the knowledge gained from recent textual discoveries. In 2001 a separate group of scholars completed the ESV. It too has its roots in the KJV family.

New Living Translation. In the 1950s Kenneth Taylor decided to create a paraphrase of the Bible for his children. Taylor knew no Greek or Hebrew, so he used the 1901 Authorized Version as the starting point for the Living Bible. This paraphrase sold so well it inspired its publisher, Tyndale House Publishers, to commission a ninety-member committee of scholars to create a dynamic equivalent in the style of the Living Bible, but using the original texts of Hebrew, Aramaic and Greek. This effort was published in 1996 as the NLT. To accommodate Taylor's original target audience of children, the NLT's authors confined their word choices to a sixth-grade reading level.

THE ADVANTAGE OF MULTIPLE TRANSLATIONS

When my children were little, we stumbled into a chocolate store one day. It was like none we had ever imagined. The place was a visual feast. Glass cases were heaped with mounds of chocolate in all shapes and sizes. There was dark chocolate and white chocolate and every flavor in between. The kids didn't walk through the store, they glided through it from one display to another, drinking in the possibilities.

The shelves of my study are stocked with dozens of different kinds of Bibles. Sometimes I glide through them like my kids in that candy store. Each version helps me understand God and his Word in slightly different ways. The Bible's original languages of Hebrew, Aramaic and Greek contain 11,280 different words. My English versions average a little less than 6,000 words each. Having multiple versions sheds light on the various nuances and shades of meaning that I could miss without them.

ASSIGNMENT

If you have access to a translation other than the one you've been using while reading *The Bible Questions*, use both versions today.

Read Psalm 1 in your usual translation, then reread it in an alternative version.

1. What do both of these versions say about the person who delights in God's law?

2. How do your translations shed different light on the person who delights in God's law?

3. What do you want to do as a result of the promises you've seen in Psalm 1?

12

Why Was God So Violent in the Old Testament?

The Father of the heavenly lights . . . does not change like shifting shadows.

The Apostle James, James 1:17

♦ ♦ ♦

In the spring of approximately 1405 B.C. the nation of Israel conquered the city of Jericho. After circling the city for seven days, the walls miraculously weakened and fell. "When the trumpets sounded, the army shouted, and at the sound of the trumpet, when the men gave a loud shout, the wall collapsed; so everyone charged straight in, and they took the city" (Joshua 6:20). If that's all that had happened, few would think twice about this battle. But the next verse reads, "They devoted the city to the LORD and destroyed with the sword every living thing in it—men and women, young and old, cattle, sheep and donkeys." The Israelites did this because of a direct command from God.

God had told them:

> In the cities of the nations the LORD your God is giving you as an inheritance, do not leave alive anything that breathes.

Completely destroy them—the Hittites, Amorites, Canaanites, Perizzites, Hivites and Jebusites—as the LORD your God has commanded you. (Deuteronomy 20:16-17)

Why was God so violent in the Old Testament? The God of the New Testament seems to be so loving and kind. What happened?

Throughout history some have posited that there are two Gods. The God of the Old Testament is different than the God of the New Testament. That's impossible since there can only be one supreme Creator. Plus, Jesus, Paul, Peter and others clearly equate the God of Abraham with the God they were following.[1]

GOD'S FULL NAME

In Exodus 34, God reveals his full name to Moses, saying, "The LORD, the LORD, the compassionate and gracious God, slow to anger, abounding in love and faithfulness, maintaining love to thousands, and forgiving wickedness, rebellion and sin. Yet he does not leave the guilty unpunished" (vv. 6-7). How could anyone "abounding in love and faithfulness" order the deaths of every man, woman, boy and girl in the city of Jericho?

God's command to put the Canaanites to death is found in Deuteronomy 20:17. He explains why they must die in verse 18: "Otherwise, they will teach you to follow all the detestable things they do in worshiping their gods, and you will sin against the LORD your God." God was building a community of people who would relate to him by faith and to one another in love. The Canaanites' worship practices were anything but loving. God did not want their infection to spread to his newly forming community of faith.

CANAAN'S WORSHIP PRACTICES

One of Canaan's gods was named *Molech*. Molech was the god of the underworld. People worshiped him by "passing their sons and daughters through the fire," a euphemism for burning their infants alive.

Baal and *Ashthoreth* were the fertility god and goddess of Canaan. Their worshipers believed that they controlled the harvest. In order to stimulate them to fertilize the land, these two needed to be aroused by viewing humans engaged in sexual activity. Worship of Baal and Ashthoreth involved temple prostitution. Parents brought their children to the temple priest to be used for this purpose.

GOD'S PATIENCE

Back up four hundred years to the time of Abraham. In Genesis 15, God makes a covenant with Abraham. "In the fourth generation your descendants will come back here, for the sin of the Amorites has not yet reached its full measure" (Genesis 15:16). Abraham was one hundred when his first child was born. So four generations was four hundred years.

For four hundred years the Amorites, Hittites, Canaanites, Perizzites and Jebusites had been sacrificing their infants to Molech and presenting their children to fertility gods for ritual prostitution. Every one of these children was precious to God the Father. According to the doctrine of the age of accountability, young children who die automatically go to heaven because they are not morally culpable. Whereas every child who grew up in this heinous, child-abusive system passed on the abusive practices to the next generation. God knew it must stop. The only way to annihilate the abuse was to annihilate the abusers.

God is patient. His character is "slow to anger, forgiving wickedness, rebellion and sin." For four hundred years he gave the peoples of Canaan the opportunity to turn from their horrible ways. The later part of his character claims, "He does not leave the guilty unpunished." In the time of Joshua, he did not leave the guilty unpunished. Instead of excising a portion of the cancer, God had it surgically removed. Otherwise, these people would have taught the Israelites to practice all the detestable activities they performed in worshiping their gods, and the Israelites would have sinned in like manner, sustaining the abuse through more generations.

The innocent Canaanite children were ushered to heaven, and the evil practices of their parents were possibly abolished. I call that a severe mercy, the best solution available for a horrible situation.

WHY GOD SEEMS MORE VIOLENT

Part of the reason God seems more violent throughout the Old Testament is because of the time span it covers. A thousand years of history passes between Moses and Malachi. The New Testament covers less than fifty years. There's simply not enough time for the same number of clashes and calamities to happen between Matthew and Revelation.

Part of the reason why God seems violent in the Old Testament is because we tend to remember bad things better than we remember good things. I'm writing this chapter a month after the city of Joplin, Missouri, experienced a cataclysmic tornado. Two months before that, a devastating earthquake struck Japan. A year prior, a major earthquake struck Chile. You may remember those disasters. I remember them vividly. Yet off the top of my head I can't recall a single positive event that happened around those same times. Why? Because we are wired for good. Good things are supposed to happen. They're the norm, so we don't mark them as deeply in our memories. Evil isn't supposed to happen. So when it does, we remember it well.

God is the same in both Testaments. He is "compassionate and gracious, . . . slow to anger, abounding in love and faithfulness, maintaining love to thousands, and forgiving wickedness, rebellion and sin. Yet he does not leave the guilty unpunished." When Adam and Eve sinned, instead of punishing them, he substituted an animal and used its skin to cover their shame. When God saw that sin was increasing on the earth, Noah found grace in his eyes. When Hagar was banished from the household of Abraham, God cared for her and her son in the desert. God cared for the Israelites in the wilderness, for Naomi and Ruth after the loss of their husbands, for Naaman when he contracted leprosy, for Elijah during the drought, for Daniel in the lion's den, for Esther in the palace, for Jonah in the belly of the whale. Much judgment went on during the Old Testament period. And much mercy too.

In the New Testament, God remained compassionate and gracious. He sent Jesus to heal the sick and proclaim freedom to the captive. Peter was rescued from prison; Paul from a shipwreck. Dorcas was given her life back. Jairus was given his daughter back. Thousands were given eternal life. During that same time, God also brought judgment on the guilty. Jesus castigated the Pharisees, drove out the money changers and pronounced judgment on Jerusalem. Ananias and Sapphira dropped dead for lying. Persecution came to the church of Jerusalem because they failed to take the initiative to fulfill the Acts 1:8 mandate.

Both the Old and New Testaments declare that God doesn't change. Psalm 102:27 says, "You remain the same, / and your years will never end." James 1:17 affirms that the Father "does not change like shifting shadows." The same God who gave birth to the universe birthed his Son on our planet. He is forever "the LORD, the LORD, the compassionate and gracious God, slow to anger, abounding in love and faithfulness, maintaining love to thousands, and forgiving wickedness, rebellion and sin. Yet he does not leave the guilty unpunished."

ASSIGNMENT
Read Exodus 34.

1. Why did God reveal his name to Moses? What was there in Moses' life that caused him to want or need to know God's name fully?

2. God's full name is "the LORD, the LORD, the compassionate and gracious God, slow to anger, abounding in love and faithfulness, maintaining love to thousands, and forgiving wickedness, rebellion and sin. Yet he does not leave the guilty unpunished." You were made in God's image. Which part of this description do you most want to live up to today?

3. God felt the need to do surgery on the land of Canaan like a surgeon removing cancer from a body. What (if any) type of surgery might the Lord want to do on your life or lifestyle in order to keep you from spreading sin or hurtfulness to your family or friends?

13

Why Is There Only
One Way to Heaven?

I am the way and the truth and the life.
No one comes to the Father except through me.

Jesus, John 14:6

◆ ◆ ◆

Not long after the church was born, the apostle Peter extended
a hand to a crippled beggar at a gate near the temple. "Silver or
gold I do not have," he said, "but what I do have I give you. In the
name of Jesus Christ of Nazareth, walk" (Acts 3:6). The beggar,
who had never taken a step in his life, jumped to his feet. As it
dawned on him what had happened, he created quite a com-
motion, jumping up and down and shouting praises to God.

People were used to singing and dancing near the temple,
but this man's exuberance attracted a crowd. Peter used the opportunity to preach the good news of Jesus to them. During his
sermon Peter boldly proclaimed, "Salvation is found in no one
else, for there is no other name under heaven given to mankind
by which we must be saved" (Acts 4:12). The city's leaders
didn't take kindly to that statement. Peter was arrested and

commanded to stop speaking in Jesus' name.

From that day to this people have taken offense at Christianity's claim that Jesus is the only way to heaven. Such a claim seems arrogant and narrow-minded. It offends people who believe otherwise.

THE ARROGANCE OF EXCLUSIVITY

We live in an age of multiple options. If I want fast food, I have no less than a dozen choices within a few miles of my home. If I want to watch television, I have almost two hundred channels to choose from. If I want to travel, I can pick from a dozen airlines and a myriad of destinations. We like choices.

We also live in an age when tolerance is a prime virtue. I may not think that what is good for you is all that good for me, but there is something wrong with me if I don't affirm your right to be different.

And then there's relativity. Your truth is your truth and my truth is my truth. To claim to have the only way to anything is the epitome of pride. How can you say you know something that's better for me than I know for myself when you've never walked in my shoes?

And yet, there it is. Christianity boldly proclaims that "Salvation is found in no one else." During his last supper, Jesus announced, "I am the way and the truth and the life. No one comes to the Father except through me" (John 14:6). The Bible teaches that there is only one way to heaven, and that is by trusting in Christ and the sin payment he made for us by his death on the cross.

How can the Bible claim to be "the good book" and make such statements?

ONE WAY IS NOT NECESSARILY ARROGANT

I pastor a church that has hundreds of young couples who produce dozens of babies annually. Pretty regularly one of these newborns will be diagnosed with jaundice. Jaundice is a buildup of something in the blood called bilirubin. I don't know exactly what that is, but it makes the baby's skin turn yellow and the parents' hearts beat fast. First-time parents sometimes panic, begging the doctor for a cure.

The doctor explains, "The cure is quite simple. We'll put your child under a blue light for a while and she [or he] will be fine in no time."

In my twenty years of pastoring I've never had a parent object to this treatment—even though they're presented with only one choice. So far, no one I know has said, "That's not fair! I want more than one option." In the case of jaundice the treatment is so simple, why would you need a second option?

The Bible teaches that Jesus Christ, God's Son, came to earth and lived a perfect life. He offered his sinless life as a substitute payment for the debt you and I have accrued because of our sins.

That may sound judgmental, but here's the truth about me: In many ways, on many occasions, I have deliberately disobeyed God. I've done things I knew were wrong at the time I was doing them. I have said things I knew weren't true to make myself look better. I have said things I knew would hurt people because I wanted to hurt them. It's God's universe, he created it. He has the right to make the rules. I have disobeyed them. I owe a debt I cannot pay. Jesus offers to pay it for me. His only stipulation is that I admit that I did those things and make a commitment to him as the Lord of my life. What could be simpler and less costly to me?

Still, this solution only presents me with one option: his way or no way. Take it or leave it. According to Christianity, I don't get any other choices. Is that fair?

COMPARING THE OPTIONS

For centuries Christianity has been so prevalent in Europe and North America that most Westerners know its claim of exclusivity. What they often don't know is that *all* major religions claim exclusivity.

A few years ago I did a study of the ten largest religions in the world. All of them offer different solutions for finding our way back to God. All of them believe in different gods and different ways of getting to him. Since they're all different, all of them can be wrong, but only one can be right.

Of all humanity 98.3 percent follow one of these ten religions. So surely, if there is a way to heaven, one of them has it. To believe otherwise is to believe in a *really* narrow way.

Here's the list, along with its number of adherents and percentage of the world's population:

1. Christianity, 2.1 billion, 33 percent of the world's population

2. Islam, 1.5 billion, 21 percent

3. Secular/nonreligious/agnostic/atheist, 1.1 billion, 16 percent

4. Hinduism, 900 million, 14 percent

5. Chinese traditional religions, 394 million, 6 percent

6. Buddhism, 376 million, 6 percent

7. Primal-Indigenous religions, 300 million, 4 percent

8. African traditional religions, 100 million, 1.5 percent

9. Sikhism, 23 million, 0.36 percent

10. Jucheism, 19 million, 0.3 percent

When we start with the assumption that *if* there is truth out there, at least five people in a thousand people will get it right, we eliminate the ninth and tenth religions right off the bat. We also eliminate Judaism, Mormonism, the Jehovah's Witnesses and Scientology. Each of these has attracted less than .25 percent of the world's population.

THE CHOICES
Let's look at the potential choices.

Jucheism is the official belief system of North Korea. All North Koreans are required to follow its teachings, which were invented by the nation's dictator Kim Il Sung. Juche teaches self-reliance. It doesn't believe in an afterlife, so in this system no one can get to heaven.

Sikhism's founder was a sixteenth-century guru named Nanak Dev Ji. Guru Nanak was troubled by the violence between Hindus and Muslims within his native province of Punjab. He blended the two religions, adopting monotheism from the Muslims and reincarnation from the Hindus. A Sikh's ultimate aim is to achieve oneness with the supreme God, making progress through practicing specific good behaviors.

Three religions on the list—African traditional religions, primal-indigenous religions and some Chinese traditional religions—are systems of animism. Animists believe that every object in the universe, from mountains to rivers to animals to rocks, is animated with a spirit and therefore should be venerated. Some animistic cultures believe in an afterlife much like life here on the earth. The Romans believed in the Elysian Fields. Native American animists subscribe to the Happy Hunting Grounds. Other animists believe in no life after death. Animists believe that their way of understanding the world is the right way.

Buddhism's founder, Siddhartha Gautama, was raised in a high-caste Hindu family. After meditating under a fig tree, he became enlightened and taught his followers to pursue a path of enlightenment by means of the Eightfold Path. Most Buddhists say that their religion is more a philosophy than a path to heaven. Many do not believe in an afterlife, while some sects believe in multiple reincarnations on a pathway to nirvana, similar to the Hinduism from which Buddhism sprang.

The majority of Chinese traditional religionists are Confucians, Shintos and Taoists. Like Buddhism, these are systems of thought and behavior rather than paths to heaven. While venerating their ancestors, most Chinese religions think of their tenets as a way of life rather than a way to heaven.

Hindus believe in multiple gods (sometimes called "avatars"), and one non-personal universal life force called "Brahman." All of life is involved with the "Brahman" and therefore, "God (the 'Brahman') is one." By living a good life, a Hindu accrues positive karma. Hindu scholars estimate that it takes around six hundred thousand reincarnated lifetimes to achieve the Hindu heaven, which is called nirvana. *Nirvana* means "blowing out." After a myriad of progressive lifetimes, when an individual's life force reaches the state of nirvana, they are melded into the cosmic energy of the universe and lose the sense of personal consciousness.

Since everyone exhibits some kind of belief system, sociologists gather many disparate groups under a banner they title "secular/ nonreligious/agnostic/atheist" peoples. The list compilers at Adherents.com admit that this is a hard group to characterize or count. Secular and nonreligious peoples claim no belief in or knowledge of an afterlife. Agnostics admit they don't know whether there is a God or an afterlife. Atheists believe there is no God or afterlife.

Islam teaches that a Muslim may achieve paradise by practicing the Five Pillars of Islam:

1. reciting the *Shahada* ("There is no god but Allah, and Mohammed is his prophet")

2. praying five times a day toward Mecca

3. giving alms to the poor

4. fasting during the daylight hours of the month of Ramadan

5. performing a pilgrimage to Mecca

The Muslim paradise is different than Christian heaven. In paradise, men lie on couches in exotic gardens while eating fine foods brought to them by beautiful maidens and enjoy other sensual pleasures.

Christianity teaches salvation by grace through faith in Christ, rather than by any works that might earn God's favor.

Each of these systems teaches that theirs is the one true religion. Each of them has a different path to a different afterlife.

According to the laws of logic, all of them could be wrong, but only one of them can be right.

ONE WAY MIGHT ACTUALLY BE A GOOD THING

I like choices. If there is only one choice, is that better than no choice at all? Since we live in God's universe, he is not required to make a way for us to get back to him. He would be within his rights to deny us any chance at eternal life. In *The God Questions* I explored this line of thinking:

- Suppose that at the beginning of time, God created human beings in his own image.

- Suppose he gave those humans free will, so they could choose for or against him.

- Suppose he created a paradise for them to live in.

- Suppose he imposed one restriction, warning them that if they violated that restriction, they would lose the gift of life he had given them.

- Suppose these people decided they disagreed with God's restriction and deliberately violated it.

- Suppose that instead of taking their lives, God forgave them and made provision for them.

- Suppose these peoples' descendants also violated God's restrictions repeatedly, hurting themselves and others.

- Suppose that God bestowed special gifts on one particular nation, so that they would know him deeply and help others break their destructive patterns.

- Suppose this chosen nation rebelled as well.

- Suppose that time after time God forgave this nation, delivering them from bad situations they created for themselves.

- Suppose that time after time God sent special messengers to communicate his love and care for them.

- Suppose these people killed the messengers.

- Suppose the people turned their backs on God, invented other religions and worshiped idols, which they carved out of stone, and animals and mountains and rivers instead of their Creator.

- Suppose, in an ultimate act of redemption, God sent his Son in a human body, not to condemn them, but to redeem them.

- Suppose, instead of welcoming him, these people rejected, tortured and killed him.

- Suppose God accepted the death of his Son as payment for the sins of the very people who put the Son to death.

- Suppose God offered his Son's murderers complete forgiveness, transcendent peace and eternal life as a free gift.

- Suppose God said, "I have only one requirement of you: that you honor my Son who gave his life for you."

If God did that, would it be fair for you to say, "God, you haven't done enough. I want another option!"

If you look at it this way, the real question isn't, Why is there only one way? but, Why is there any way at all?

ASSIGNMENT
Read Acts 4:1-21.

1. How strongly did Peter believe that Jesus was the only way?

2. What caused Peter to have such a strong belief?

3. What causes you to believe what you believe about Jesus?

14

When Will Jesus Return?

*He must remain in heaven until
the time for the final restoration of all things,
as God promised long ago through his holy prophets.*

The Apostle Peter, Acts 3:21 (NLT)

♦ ♦ ♦

In September 1992, Family Radio Worldwide's president Harold Camping released a book titled *1994*. In it, Camping predicted that Jesus would return that year. By the spring of 2011, Camping was at it again, predicting Christ's return on May 21, 2011. Camping is not the first to set a date for the return of Christ, and he won't be the last.

- In A.D. 51 the Thessalonian Christians began to believe that Jesus' return was imminent. Some quit their jobs and may have even taken to camping on hillsides awaiting him.

- In A.D. 90 Clement I predicted the world would end at any moment.

- During the second century Montanus and his prophetesses predicted Jesus' return in their lifetime.

- In 365 Hilary of Poitiers predicted the end of the world.

- Sextus Julius Africanus predicted Armageddon would occur in 500.

- An eclipse in 968 led some to believe that the world would end soon under the army of German Otto III.

- Many Christians believed that Christ would return on Jan. 1, 1000. Others said it would happen in 1033, a thousand years after his resurrection.

- Dozens more such prophecies occurred during the Middle Ages and the Renaissance.

- In modern times Joseph Smith, founder of the Mormon faith, recorded a vision in which he was told, "Joseph, my son, if thou livest until thou art eighty-five years old, thou shalt see the face of the Son of Man; therefore let this suffice, and trouble me no more on this matter."[1]

- *Watchtower*, the official communiqué of the Jehovah's Witnesses, has predicted the return of Christ in 1914, 1915, 1918, 1920, 1925, 1941, 1975 and 1994.

WHEN HE WILL COME

Lots of embarrassment could have been avoided if these well-meaning people had believed the words of Jesus when he said, "About that day or hour no one knows, not even the angels in heaven, nor the Son, but only the Father. Be on guard! Be alert! You do not know when that time will come" (Mark 13:32-33). Jesus communicated that he would come "at an hour when you do not expect him" (Matthew 24:44). In support of this, Paul taught that "the day of the Lord will come like a thief in the night" (1 Thessalonians 5:2).

A FORESHADOWING

That said, a growing number of students of Jewish culture believe that Jesus will return on the festival of Yom T'ruah. *Yom T'ruah* means a "day of blowing." It is also called the feast of trumpets.[2] The feast takes place on Tishri 1. Its more popular name is Rosh Hashanah, the Jewish New Year.

Tishri 1 is the first day of the seventh month of the Hebrew calendar. The grain harvest is to be completed on that day, so this is a day of harvest celebration. Jews sometimes refer to this day as "the day no one knows." Why? In ancient times Jews lived by a lunar calendar. The new year must begin with a new moon, attested by at least two witnesses. The priests in the temple would look into the sky to determine if the new moon had appeared. Until this happened, no one knew for sure whether this was the day, or whether the new moon would begin the following day.

If there were enough witnesses the official announcement of the new year was made following morning prayer. A shofar blower would climb to the highest level of the temple and blow a series of short blasts, long blasts and staccato blasts to announce the feast of trumpets.

The staccato blasts were like an alarm to alert troops of danger and call them to arms. The long final blast signified victory. This blast is "the last trumpet" (1 Corinthians 15:52).

The shofar was blown in each of the four directions of the compass. The shofar is not a brass trumpet, it's a ram's horn. It has a finite range. To make sure everyone in Israel heard the shofar's summons, a relay of shofar blowers were stationed at intervals throughout the land. When these men heard the long and short blasts indicating the first of Tishri had arrived, they turned and sounded their trumpets in all four directions as well. This was repeated until the sound of the shofar was heard throughout every portion of the land. Hence the phrase *a day of blowing*.[3]

When a person heard the trumpet blast, he or she was to immediately start out for the assembly in Jerusalem. The person was not to go back into his or her house, even for a cloak (Matthew 24:17-18).

Imagine if this festival is the foreshadowing of what will happen on the day of Christ's return. Trumpets will be heard in staccato blasts all over the earth, one after another after another!

Then, with one final blast, Christ will return and assemble his people in Jerusalem!

HOW JESUS WILL COME

No one knows when Jesus will come, but we know a fair amount about how he will come. He told us in John 14:3, "I will come back." So he will return *personally*. He also said, "As lightning that comes from the east is visible even in the west, so will be the coming of the Son of Man" (Matthew 24:27). So he will be coming *publicly*. The apostle Paul tells us Jesus will come, "In a flash, in the twinkling of an eye, at the last trumpet" (1 Corinthians 15:52). So he will be coming *quickly*. The angels who attended his ascension told the disciples that Jesus will return "in the same way you have seen him go into heaven" (Acts 1:11). So he will return *bodily*. And Hebrews 9:28 reveals his purpose in returning. "He will appear a second time, not to bear sin, but to bring salvation to those who are waiting for him."

FOUR KEY PASSAGES

The most prominent New Testament passages that speak of the Lord's return are 1-2 Thessalonians, Matthew 24–25 and the book of Revelation. The Thessalonians were initially concerned that their believing friends who had died would miss Christ's return. Paul wrote 1 Thessalonians to assure them that "the dead in Christ will rise first" (1 Thessalonians 4:16). From this we know that the resurrection of all deceased Christians will take place at the return of Christ. This is the first of two resurrections. The second resurrection takes place at the end of the millennium. The millennium is the one-thousand-year period of time in which Christ will reign on the earth in bodily form (Revelation 20:3). At the close of the millennium, all who have died without Christ will be resurrected and face final judgment.

In 2 Thessalonians the church was worried that they had

somehow missed Christ's coming. Paul wrote a second time to assure them that Christ's return will follow the rebellion of "the lawless one," who "will use all sorts of displays of power through signs and wonders that serve the lie, and all the ways that wickedness deceives those who are perishing" (2 Thessalonians 2:9-10).

In Matthew 24–25 Jesus lists several events that must take place before he returns. The most significant of these is that "this gospel of the kingdom will be preached . . . to all nations" (Matthew 24:14). This does not mean that everyone will become a Christian or even that everyone will personally hear the gospel preached. Jesus said, "This gospel . . . will be preached in the whole world, . . . and then the end will come." Within each ethnic group and each region of the world, the gospel will be proclaimed.

In this same passage Jesus describes an increase in wars, famines, earthquakes and false prophets, calling these "birth pangs"—early warning signs that his return isn't far off. His final sign is the darkening of the sun, moon and stars. When that happens, they will "see the Son of Man coming on the clouds of heaven, with power and great glory" (Matthew 24:30).

The book of Revelation gives the most vivid description of the Lord's return. With the armies of the world gathered for the battle of Armageddon, John says, "I saw heaven standing open and there before me was a white horse, whose rider is called Faithful and True. With justice he judges and wages war. His eyes are like blazing fire, and on his head are many crowns" (Revelation 19:11-12). John records, "The armies of heaven were following him, riding on white horses and dressed in fine linen, white and clean. Coming out of his mouth is a sharp sword with which to strike down the nations" (vv. 14-15). "The beast and the kings of the earth and their armies [were] gathered together to wage war against the rider on the horse and his army" (v. 19). I believe that the "sword" that comes out of Jesus' mouth is figurative, since he is the living Word. With his words he defeats the forces of evil and then establishes his kingdom here on the earth for a thousand years (Revelation 19:20–20:2).

COULD JESUS RETURN AT ANY MOMENT?

Jesus' final words in the Bible are, "I am coming soon" (Revelation 22:20). In many other places, the Bible warns believers to "be ready, because the Son of Man will come at an hour when you do not expect him" (Matthew 24:44; Luke 12:40; see also Mark 13:33). James says, "The Lord's coming is near" (James 5:8). Peter says, "The end of all things is near" (1 Peter 4:7). Does this mean Jesus might come at any moment?

Some Bible scholars believe Jesus can't return immediately because of the signs that have yet to be fulfilled. Others believe it's possible that all the critical signs have already been fulfilled. The most important fulfillment is the preaching of the gospel to all nations. Walt Wilson, founder of Global Media Outreach, tells me that the world will be blanketed by cell phone coverage by 2015. At that time, the whole world will have the gospel preached to them twenty-four hours a day via bytes. Might the end come then?[4]

I am neither a prophet nor the son of a prophet (and I work for a nonprofit institution), but I believe that Jesus may well return within our lifetime. Yet I concede that every generation since the resurrection has believed that Jesus might return in their lifetime.

WHY THE AMBIGUITY?

The way the Bible's second-coming prophecies have been written leaves Bible students with a lot of ambiguity. The Bible seems to indicate that Jesus might come soon, but he might not come for several hundred years. Since Scripture is so clear on so many issues, why is it so murky on this one?

I believe the Lord has deliberately veiled the timing of his return in mystery. During the periods in history when a Montanus or a Harold Camping rally people to think that Christ is returning within a few months, some people have quit working on long-term projects. Their reasoning is, if Jesus is coming in a few days or weeks, what's the point in building a road or a house that will never be used? Why research cancer if the world will end before I have time to find the cure?

On the other hand, Christ followers who believe that Jesus might return within a few months tend to live with a sense of urgency. They reason that if this is our last week on earth, we want to make sure we live righteously and do everything we can to share God's good news with our friends and neighbors.

Sometimes tension is a good thing. This is one of those cases. Knowing that Christ might return soon motivates us to short-term action. Knowing that he might delay for many years gives us incentive to accomplish long-term goals.

ASSIGNMENT

After explaining the signs leading up to his return in Matthew 24, Jesus told three parables about how to prepare for his return. Read the parable of the bags of gold in Matthew 25:14-30.

1. What are the two phrases the master uses with his servants (vv. 21, 23, 26)?

2. What is Jesus' point in telling this parable?

3. What will you do today with what you know about this parable and about Christ's return?

15

Where Is the Trinity Found
in Scripture?

Holy , holy, holy! Lord God Almighty!
All Thy works shall praise Thy name in earth and sky and sea;
Holy, holy, holy! Merciful and mighty!
God in three persons, blessed Trinity.

Reginald Heber

♦ ♦ ♦

Shortly after Constantine legalized Christianity throughout the
Roman Empire, a theological controversy developed in Alexandria, Egypt. A pastor named Arius began teaching that the Son
of God was a created being.[1] Arius insisted, "The Son has a beginning, but . . . God is without beginning." His bishop, Alex-
ander, excommunicated him and banished him from the church.

Whether or not the Son had a beginning might seem like a
minor issue, but it has tremendous implications. If the Son was a
created being who created beings who also created beings, the
universe would be exactly the way the Gnostics described it: a
universe of successively higher orders of gods and demigods, one
emanating from another.

Arius had a flare for public relations. He put his false theology into jingles, much like our television commercials. They stuck in peoples' minds. Well-packaged "spin" can sometimes be more persuasive than simply stated truth. Arius gained such a following that Emperor Constantine got involved. In A.D. 325, the emperor convened an ecumenical council of the church. He invited three hundred bishops to the town of Nicaea to discuss and decide the issue of Christ's preexistence and his relationship to God the Father.

Constantine presided over the opening sessions of the council. He reminded those present that division in the church is worse than war. The council settled the issue by affirming a creed that became known as the Creed of Nicaea.

The bishops of Nicaea read Scripture carefully in order to put together this creed. You would think that a statement issued by several hundred powerful men of the church would have ended the debate forever. It didn't. The controversy continued for the next fifty years, finally being settled by three brilliant minds at a second council, the First Council of Constantinople, in A.D. 381. The leading theologians at Constantinople were Gregory of Nazianzus, Gregory of Nyssa and Basil the Great. Together they are known as the Cappadocian Fathers. Cappadocia was a region of central Anatolia, in modern-day Turkey.

The Cappadocians helped the church clarify our understanding of the three persons of the Godhead not as three distinctly different beings, but three personal disclosures of God that correspond to what he is really like. The formal statement we have come to adopt is that "the one God exists in three Persons and one substance, distinctly coexisting in unity as co-equal, co-eternal, and consubstantial, or of one being."[2] The creed that was finally affirmed is called the Nicene Creed.

We believe in one God, the Father Almighty, maker of heaven and earth, and of all things visible and invisible.

And in one Lord Jesus Christ, the only-begotten Son of God, begotten of the Father before all worlds; God of God, Light of Light, very God of very God; begotten, not made, being of one substance with the Father, by whom all things were made. Who, for us men and for our salvation, came down from heaven, and was incarnate by the Holy Spirit of the virgin Mary, and was made man; and was crucified also for us under Pontius Pilate; he suffered and was buried; and the third day he rose again, according to the Scriptures; and ascended into heaven, and sits on the right hand of the Father; and he shall come again, with glory, to judge the quick and the dead; whose kingdom shall have no end.

And in the Holy Ghost, the Lord and Giver of Life; who proceeds from the Father and the Son; who with the Father and the Son together is worshiped and glorified; who spoke by the prophets; and in one holy catholic and apostolic church.

We acknowledge one baptism for the remission of sins.

We look for the resurrection of the dead, and the life of the world to come. Amen.

HOW THE TRINITY RELATE TO ONE ANOTHER

The second paragraph of the creed describes the Son as "begotten" of the Father (*monogenēs*). This is the word used in John 1:14, 18 in the King James Version. The third paragraph describes the Holy Spirit as "proceeding" from the Father and the Son. In John 15:26, "When the helper comes, whom I shall send to you from the Father, the Spirit of truth who proceeds [*ekporeuetai*] from the Father, he will testify of Me" (NKJV). Therefore, theologians speak of the Father "begetting" the Son and the Spirit "proceeding" from the Father and the Son. How the Trinity exactly interacts is a mystery, so instead of attempting to explain it, the Nicene fathers elected to restrict themselves to the words used in the Scriptures.

THE TRINITY IN SCRIPTURE

There are two reasons it took the church so long to clarify the issue of God's nature. One is our lack of experience. As finite beings it is hard to comprehend an infinite Creator. Explaining God is like explaining the concept of depth to a two-dimensional creature. We have no experience with things beyond ourselves.

The second reason it's hard to articulate the Trinity is because the word *Trinity* isn't mentioned in the Bible.

Though Scripture never mentions the word *Trinity*, it clearly teaches the existence of Father, Son and Holy Spirit as fully God, with all that means in terms of power, personality and eternal coexistence. In certain passages we even see the Trinity interacting as one.

The opening verses of Genesis show the Father creating by means of the word, while the Holy Spirit witnessed the creation first hand. "Now the earth was formless and empty, darkness was over the surface of the deep, and the Spirit of God was hovering over the waters. And God said, 'Let there be light,' and there was light" (Genesis 1:2-3). God the Father speaks (through the Word) while the Spirit hovers over creation.

In Genesis 1:26, God speaks in the plural. "Let us make mankind in our image, in our likeness." When we were made, lo and behold, we were created male and female—a unity in diversity.

So God created mankind in his own image,
    in the image of God he created them;
    male and female he created them. (v. 27)

God is a unity in diversity. We reflect God's image in that there are two expressions of us (male and female), which are both fully human. One without the other is not a full expression of humankind.

The Trinity is seen interacting at Jesus' baptism in Matthew 3:16-17: "As soon as Jesus was baptized, he went up out of the water.

At that moment was heaven opened, and he saw the Spirit of God descending like a dove and alighting on him. And a voice from heaven said, 'This is my Son, whom I love; with him I am well pleased.' "

The Trinity is mentioned together in the baptismal formula Jesus gave as part of his Great Commission: "Go and make disciples of all nations, baptizing them in the name of the Father and of the Son and of the Holy Spirit" (Matthew 28:19). All three are also together in Paul's benediction in 2 Corinthians 13:14: "May the grace of the Lord Jesus Christ, and the love of God, and the fellowship of the Holy Spirit be with you all."

OTHER HINTS

The Jews' most famous creed is Deuteronomy 6:4: "Hear, O Israel: The LORD our God, the LORD is one." The word *one* here is *echad*, which means "one" in a collective sense. God is an essential unity, just as Adam and Eve became "one [*echad*] flesh" in Genesis 2:24. The large cluster of grapes brought back by the twelve spies was "a single [*echad*] cluster."

In Isaiah 48:16 the anointed One (Jesus) seems to be speaking as he says, "And now the Sovereign LORD has sent me, / endowed with his Spirit."

ANALOGIES

The Trinity is a humbling doctrine. It reminds us that God is God, and we can't fully explain him. A few analogies have been used, but they are incomplete. The two most common analogies are the egg, whose shell, white and yoke all are egg, but only together do they fully represent eggness. And water, whose three states—solid, liquid and steam—are all fully water, but not completely water without the presence of all three states together. The fact that water can exist in three different states and still be water tells us it is possible for one being to exist in three different "states" or "persons" and still be one in substance.

ASSIGNMENT

Read Matthew 3:13-17.

1. How does the Father feel about the Son?

2. Why did the Spirit choose that moment to descend on Jesus?

3. What made Jesus' baptism so important that all three members of the Trinity were present?

PART FOUR

Practical Questions

It is out of the Word of God that a system
has come to make life sweet.

Benjamin Harrison

16

How Do I Study the Bible?

I have always said, and will always say, that the studious perusal
of the sacred volume will make better homes, better citizens,
better fathers and better husbands.

Thomas Jefferson

♦ ♦ ♦

Daniel was dragged into captivity during his teenage years and spent his life growing up and serving in the courts of Babylon. In his twenties he became the prime minister, serving multiple kings in this capacity. At the ripe old age of eighty-seven, he journaled about his personal experience with Scripture.

> In the first year of Darius son of Xerxes . . . I, Daniel, understood from the Scriptures, according to the word of the LORD given to Jeremiah the prophet, that the desolation of Jerusalem would last seventy years. So I turned to the Lord God and pleaded with him in prayer and petition, in fasting, and in sackcloth and ashes. (Daniel 9:1-3)

From this we learn that Daniel read the Bible regularly and took it very personally.

On this particular day, Daniel was reading Jeremiah 29. There

God says, "When seventy years are completed for Babylon, I will come to you and fulfill my good promise to bring you back to this place" (v. 10). As Daniel was reading, he got out his abacus and realized that Israel had been in exile for almost seventy years. It was time to go home! As was his habit, he did more than just read the Scriptures, he applied what he learned by praying that God would fulfill the prophecy he had just read.

Since ancient times, people have made life-altering discoveries by studying the Bible. Unfortunately, far too many Christians restrict God's access to their hearts by limiting their intake of God's Word to the Sunday morning sermon. This kind of diet leaves people biblically malnourished and often critical. They expect their pastor to feed them all the spiritual calories they need for the week, in forty-five minutes or less.

CRAVE IT

The apostle Peter encourages Christians, "Like newborn babies, crave pure spiritual milk, so that by it you may grow up in your salvation" (1 Peter 2:2). Observe three things in this verse.

First, *your appetite for the Bible ought to be like a newborn baby looking for its next meal.* When our son Bryan was three months old, Lori resumed her graduate studies. Once a week she made an hour's trek to Denver Seminary to work on her master's degree. I was left at home with bottles of milk and the task of taking care of our little bundle for the evening.

The first night this happened, I was unprepared for Bryan's voracious appetite. At the proper time I removed a bottle from the freezer and started warming it in a pan of water. The milk was still frozen when Bryan began to whimper. I turned the flame up under the pan and tried to comfort him with some gentle rocking, to no avail. His whimpering became whining, then howling, then wailing. In desperation I took the half-frozen bottle out of the water and inserted the nipple in his mouth. I figured this frigid liquid would shock him and give me more time to put it back in the water and heat it up properly.

Not a chance! He consumed that bottle like a vulture on a dead antelope. Within minutes the liquid was in his stomach and all that remained was the big frozen ice ball in the middle of the bottle. He must have been experiencing brain freeze from all that cold milk, but he only fussed for more.

As quick as I could, I put the bottle back in the water and took a second bottle from the freezer, for good measure. As fast as I could heat those things, his little lips downed them like they were his last meal. My little newborn had an appetite for milk!

Besides having a newborn's appetite, Peter also says, we ought to "*crave* pure spiritual milk." Babies don't think too far ahead, but we age, we're able to anticipate a good meal. The apostle's point is, we ought to look forward to reading and studying the Bible like a pregnant woman craves a bowl of ice cream or a gourmet pizza.

Such desire doesn't happen instantly. God's Word is an acquired taste. Psalm 19:10 says the words of God are sweeter than honey. Yet many of us shy away from it like it is soured milk. People who learn to study the Bible for themselves can't imagine *not* reading it regularly. But many people never spend enough time in it to acquire that kind of taste. This is a shame of the highest magnitude.

Peter's third piece of advice is that we *study* the Bible so we can grow up. Notice, he is not saying the purpose of Bible study is to *know* more but to *grow* more. The Bible's purpose is to teach, rebuke, correct and train us in righteousness (2 Timothy 3:16). Not to fill our brain with simple biblical facts, but to fill it with God's perspective and transform our life.

Over the next five chapters, I want to teach you how to study the Bible in a way that is addictive, so that you crave the pure milk of God's Word.

HOW TO STUDY THE BIBLE

If you've ever listened to a great Bible teacher you've probably wondered, *Where did he (or she) get those insights? How did she (or he) discover all that in the text?* Chances are they followed a three-step process. The process is a time-tested one; it progresses from *observation* to *interpretation* to *application.*

If you will follow this simple three-step system, your life will be transformed on a daily basis.

As I open my Bible each morning, I ask the Lord to guide me to insights that will feed my soul, increase my character or enable me to serve others more effectively. I then turn to wherever I left off my reading the day before. With the possible exception of Psalms and Proverbs, every book of the Bible was meant to be read from start to finish. If I'm reading a narrative section of the Bible (usually one of the books of history, though prophetic books have stories in them too), I read an entire story. If I'm reading in one of the New Testament Epistles, I usually read a chapter (but sometimes just a paragraph). If I'm reading wisdom or prophetic literature, I read whatever seems like a logical unit of thought. I read the whole section through to see what's there, like a scout investigating the trail ahead of his troops. Then I get out my pen to write and reflect.

OBSERVATION: WHAT DOES THE TEXT SAY?

The first step I take is to determine what's in the text. This is the *observation* phase of my study. Observation asks the question, What does the text say? It's amazing how simple that question seems, and how much we miss until we ask it.

I write down my observations, then move to step two, which is *interpretation.* Interpretation asks, What does the text mean? I record my interpretation, and then move to step three. *Application* asks, What am I going to do about this?

We'll cover interpretation and application in the next two chapters. For now, let's concentrate on learning to observe.

Rudyard Kipling wrote a poem that reminds me of the six questions I ask while observing the text.

I keep six honest serving-men,
(They taught me all I knew.)
Their names are What and Why and When
And How and Where and Who.
I send them over land and sea,
I send them east and west;
But after they have worked for me,
I give them all a rest.[1]

A keen observer approaches the text of Scripture like Sherlock Holmes does a crime scene. They ask, Who did this? What went on here? When did it happen? Where did they come from? How did it unfold like this? Why is this particular passage included in Scripture? The six questions *who, what, when, where, how* and *why* are your best friends during step one. The more questions you ask, the more you'll see in the text.

We live in a fast-paced culture. It's hard for us to slow down to see what's going on around us, much less to slow down long enough to see what's happened in a book like the Bible. Doing so opens a whole new world. Like walking along a trail, we see things that were always there but we never paused to observe.

POWERS OF OBSERVATION

Great teachers know that students learn more when they make discoveries for themselves. This is the major difference between *being* fed and *feeding yourself.* When I make an observation for the people in my church, they're impressed. When I help them make observations for themselves, they're blessed (pardon the rhyme). The good (and bad) news is, the only way to learn to make observations is to make some for yourself.

Learning to make observations. During my sophomore year of college I was introduced to a story called "The Student, the Fish, and Agassiz." It's a real story that sheds brilliant light on the skill of making observations. The student was Samuel Scudder, an aspiring scientist who was beginning his study of natural history at Harvard University. Agassiz was the famous Dr. Louis Agassiz, a Swiss-born paleontologist. The fish was a Haemulon. I later found out that the common name for Haemulon is a "grunt."[2]

Upon entering Dr. Agassiz's laboratory, Scudder was handed a pan with a Haemulon in it, basted in alcohol. His assignment was to make as many observations as possible of the fish. In Scudder's own words:

> In ten minutes I had seen all that could be seen in that fish, and started in search of the Professor—who had, however, left the Museum; and when I returned . . . nothing was to be done but to return to a steadfast gaze at my mute companion. Half an hour passed—an hour—another hour; the fish began to look loathsome. I turned it over and around; looked it in the face—ghastly; from behind, beneath, above, sideways, at a three-quarters' view—just as ghastly. I was in despair; at an early hour I concluded that lunch was necessary; so, with infinite relief, the fish was carefully replaced in the jar, and for an hour I was free.
>
> On my return, I learned that Professor Agassiz had been at the Museum, but had gone, and would not return for several hours. . . . Slowly I drew forth that hideous fish, and with a feeling of desperation again looked at it. I might not use a magnifying-glass; instruments of all kinds were interdicted. My two hands, my two eyes, and the fish: it seemed a most limited field. I pushed my finger down its throat to feel how sharp the teeth were. I began to count the scales in the different rows, until I was convinced that that was nonsense. At last a happy thought struck me—I would draw the fish;

and now with surprise I began to discover new features in the creature. Just then the Professor returned.

"That is right," said he; "a pencil is one of the best of eyes. I am glad to notice, too, that you keep your specimen wet, and your bottle corked."

With these encouraging words, he added, "Well, what is it like?"

He listened attentively to my brief rehearsal of the structure of parts whose names were still unknowns to me: the fringed gill-arches and movable *operculum*; the pores of the head, fleshy lips and lidless eyes; the lateral line, the spinous fins and forked tail; the compressed and arched body. When I finished, he waited as if expecting more, and then, with an air of disappointment, "You have not looked very carefully; why," he continued more earnestly, "you haven't even seen one of the most conspicuous features of the animal, which is as plainly before your eyes as the fish itself; look again, look again!" and he left me to my misery.

I was piqued; I was mortified. Still more of that wretched fish! But now I set myself to my task with a will, and discovered one new thing after another, until I saw how just the Professor's criticism had been. The afternoon passed quickly; and when, towards its close, the Professor inquired, "Do you see it yet?"

"No," I replied, "I am certain I do not, but I see how little I saw before."

"That is next best," said he, earnestly, "but I won't hear you now; put away your fish and go home; perhaps you will be ready with a better answer in the morning. I will examine you before you look at the fish."

This was disconcerting. Not only must I think of my fish all night, studying, without the object before me, what this unknown but most visible feature might be; but also, without reviewing my discoveries, I must give an exact account of them the next day. I had a bad memory; so I walked home by Charles River in a distracted state, with my two perplexities.

The cordial greeting from the Professor the next morning was reassuring; here was a man who seemed to be quite as anxious as I that I should see for myself what he saw. "Do you perhaps mean," I asked, "that the fish has symmetrical sides with paired organs?"

His thoroughly pleased "Of course! Of course!" repaid the wakeful hours of the previous night. After he had discoursed most happily and enthusiastically—as he always did—upon the importance of this point, I ventured to ask what I should do next. "Oh, look at your fish!" he said, and left me again to my own devices. In a little more than an hour he returned, and heard my new catalogue.

"That is good, that is good!" he repeated; "but that is not all; go on" and so for three long days he placed that fish before my eyes, forbidding me to look at anything else, or to use any artificial aid. "Look, look, look," was his repeated injunction.

This was the best entomological lesson I ever had—a lesson whose influence has extended to the details of every subsequent study; a legacy the Professor had left to me, as he has left it to many others, of inestimable value, which we could not buy, with which we cannot part.

While Scudder makes observation sound like a tedious chore, it's really not. It's more like an adventurer exploring new territory to discover what's there. Every step you take, every place your eye lands is new and exciting.

Another way to think of observation is like the salad of biblical study. It provides the roughage that will keep you regular and help you digest all you take in thereafter. It's the first of a three-course meal. In my personal Bible time, if I have a half hour, I'll spend ten minutes reading, ten minutes writing observations, five minutes interpreting and two to three minutes writing my application. If I have an hour, I'll double that. If fifteen minutes, I cut it in half.

ASSIGNMENT

Read Acts 2:41-47. Here I have given you five examples of observations from this passage. Read through them. Then take a sheet of paper or spiral notebook, and write down at least ten observations to add to the list. You should be able to do this in under ten minutes. For a bigger challenge, make twenty-five observations. For a really big challenge, go for fifty! Keep your list; you'll want to use it again with the coming chapters.

Observations of Acts 2:41-47:

1. Someone took the time to count how many had been baptized and joined the church (v. 41).

2. In this great church the new believers were so zealous for their faith that they didn't merely attend meetings and go through motions, they *devoted* themselves to the things of the Lord (v. 42).

3. The four activities they devoted themselves to (teaching, fellowship, breaking of bread, prayer) are spiritual habits that increased their faith (v. 42).

4. God's Spirit was free to work miracles in their midst (v. 43).

5. There was a spirit of generosity among the believers (vv. 44-45).

17

How Do I Find the
Meaning of the Text?

In Observation, we excavate. In Interpretation, we erect.

Howard Hendricks

♦ ♦ ♦

Several years ago I read Acts 2:42-47, camping on the final verse: "And the Lord added to their number daily those who were being saved." I observed that if one person a day were coming to Christ, the Jerusalem church was seeing at least 365 people come to Christ every year.

My next step was *interpretation*. If observation answers the question, What does the text say? interpretation answers, What does the text mean? When I write an interpretation, I try to compose a timeless principle based on the point I've observed in the text. I believe Acts 2 is not a description of the *ideal* church but of a *normal* church acting in the power of the Spirit. So my interpretation for Acts 2:47 was, *God wants his church to grow by adding new believers on a regular basis.*

As I noted that, I whispered under my breath, "Lord, someday I would like to be part of a church that averaged a person a day coming to Christ." The previous year, New Song Community Church had seen fifty-three people indicate decisions for Christ, an average of one every seven days. That year, we saw an average of one decision every six days. The following year, we witnessed a decision every five days. The average increased like that until the year we saw a person a day come to Christ. As I'm writing these words, we are averaging seeing four people a day give their lives to Christ.

Would God have led New Song to such fruitfulness if I hadn't prayed that prayer? I don't know. Sometimes he uses us in spite of ourselves. More often, though, he acts in response to our prayers. I do know that my "Lord, someday" prayer would not have happened if I hadn't been studying Scripture that day. I also know that if I had just been reading for content rather than meaning, I might have missed the principle that has led our church to see so many salvations.

OBSERVATION WITHOUT INTERPRETATION

Making observations is the first step in personal Bible study. It can be an exhilarating time of collecting facts. But facts don't change the way we live. *Principles* point us toward life change. Principles are the key to biblical application.

Some types of Scripture are already in principle form. The book of Proverbs is pretty much one principle after another. Many verses in the New Testament letters are in principle form too. But the stories, parables, poetry and prophecy of the Bible need to be gleaned: What point is this particular passage making? That's the principle. The purpose of Scripture isn't just to educate us but to edify us. To conform us increasingly into the likeness of God's Son.

That's where interpretation comes in. Observation without interpretation is like scouting the opposing team and then playing as if we knew nothing about them. The point of observing our opponents is to take note of their strengths, weaknesses and tendencies, and then play a better game.

Fact: David defeated Goliath. That's encouraging, but what do we learn from it that can make us play better next time we're up against some ungodly competition?

Fact: Esther prayed and fasted before she went to see the king. What principle do we see in her story that will make us better servants the next time people we love are facing danger?

AN INTERPRETATION IS A TIMELESS PRINCIPLE

A *principle* is a basic truth or law that describes how God, life or the world works on a normal basis. To be *timeless* means to be outside of or removed from time. A *timeless principle* is something that is true about the way things work in a variety of situations and settings.

When we find a timeless principle, we've tapped into a vein of gold. A timeless principle applies as well to our situation and circumstances as it did to the people in the Bible. Here are a few examples.

Observation. David killed Goliath with a stone, a sling and a belief that God would enable him to triumph over his enemy.

Timeless principle. With faith, it is possible to overcome incredible odds.

Observation. Esther fasted for a responsive heart from the king.

Timeless principle. Fasting is a tool to utilize when circumstances call for a miracle.

Ezekiel 46 gives a description of how things are supposed to happen in the temple. Verse 9 says,

> When the people of the land come before the LORD at the appointed festivals, whoever enters by the north gate to worship is to go out the south gate; and whoever enters by the south gate is to go out the north gate. No one is to return through the gate by which they entered, but each is to go out the opposite gate.

What's the point?

One simple observation: When God's people come for worship, they should leave differently than how they came in.

The timeless principle? Every time you come for worship, determine to leave changed.

MOVING FROM OBSERVATION TO INTERPRETATION

In your personal Bible study, once you've made some observations, ask three questions of each of them:

1. What's the point? (This will steer you toward a principle.)

2. In what way is this true today? (This will steer you toward timelessness.)

3. In what way is this true in my cultural setting? (This is a second check for timelessness.)

These simple questions will get you thinking on a higher level. As you make interpretations, write them down.

CHECK YOURSELF

Next, check yourself by asking a few more questions:

1. Does this principle seem true to what God is saying in this passage?

2. Does it seem true to what God teaches elsewhere in Scripture? (The Bible does not contradict itself.)

3. Is this principle almost always true? (Principles, by nature, are not laws. There can be exceptions to them.)

4. Is this principle a way of seeing the world or doing life in conformity to God's ways?

If your answer to all of these is yes, you've got a great interpretation. If not, you may need to tweak, refine or reword your concept. This is called *thinking*, and thinking is hard work! This is part of what it means to love God with your mind.

EXAMPLES

More examples may help. In chapter sixteen I listed five observations from Acts 2:41-47. A single observation can sometimes point us to more than one principle, so I've given two examples of principles for each observation here.

- *Observation.* Someone took the time to count how many had been baptized and joined the church (v. 41).

  Principle 1. Healthy churches don't happen by accident. They plan and pay attention to details.

  Principle 2. The number of people who come to Christ and join the church matters to God.

- *Observation.* In this great church the new believers were so zealous for their faith that they didn't merely attend meetings and go through motions, they *devoted* themselves to the things of the Lord (v. 42).

  Principle 1. Serious Christians take church attendance seriously.

  Principle 2. Church leaders should pray for and inspire devotion in their members.

- *Observation.* The four activities they devoted themselves to (teaching, fellowship, breaking of bread, prayer) are spiritual habits that will increase our faith (v. 42).

  Principle 1. Healthy churches design and teach deliberate habits for spiritual growth.

  Principle 2. Fellowship is so important that the church should develop a system where everyone can experience it personally.

- *Observation.* God's Spirit was free to work miracles in their midst (v. 43).

  Principle 1. Miracles may not happen regularly in every church, but every church ought to experience awe and wonder.

Principle 2. Members should pray for God's Spirit to work in their church.

- *Observation.* There was a spirit of generosity among the believers (v. 45).

Principle 1. Generosity is a hallmark of sincere believers.

Principle 2. Generosity fuels ministry.

Notice that none of these principles requires you to actually *do* anything. They point you toward something worth doing. *Doing* comes in the application phase. We'll tackle that in the next chapter. In the meantime, if you'd like a list of good observation and interpretation questions, I've included a few in appendix one.

WHAT YOU THINK ABOUT IS WHAT YOU BECOME

Working this process from observation to interpretation will not only help you mine nuggets of truth from God's Word, it is part of the process of being transformed by the renewing of your mind. While you are developing and refining principles, you are thinking deeply about the truths of Scripture. This, in itself, is one of the most helpful ways to develop a deep spiritual life. The principle behind this is, *What you think about is what you eventually become.*

ASSIGNMENT

Reread Acts 2:41-47. The best way to learn to interpret Scripture is to practice interpreting Scripture. Take the list of observations you made from this passage (see assignment in chap. 16) and develop a timeless principle for each one. This may take some work! When you're done you'll feel great about the thinking you've done. This is part of what it means to be washed by the Word (Ephesians 5:26).

18

How Do I Apply What I Learn?

Application is what got the Prophets killed.

Haddon Robinson

♦ ♦ ♦

Ezra the scribe is one of my heroes. How he lived his life is how I want to live mine. In Ezra 7:9 we learn that "the gracious hand of his God was on him." Most people would trade their left elbow to be able to say that. What was Ezra's secret? How did he warrant God's gracious hand? Ezra tells us in the next verse: "Ezra had devoted himself to the study and observance of the Law of the LORD, and to teaching its decrees and laws."

Notice the order. Step one: study it. Step two: practice it. Step three: teach it. A lot of well-meaning people never get around to studying the Bible. They don't have time, or they don't know how. Fortunately, you now know a significant method for studying God's Word. The method isn't quite complete though, and that's where Ezra's order comes in. After studying God's law, he determined to put it into practice. Only after personally applying the Word to his own life did Ezra feel qualified to move into a teaching ministry.

The book of James makes a prescient observation about Bible study that's void of application. "Anyone who listens to the word but does not do what it says is like someone who looks at his face in a mirror and, after looking at himself, goes away and immediately forgets what he looks like" (James 1:23-24). Translated: "What's the point of looking at Scripture at all if you're not going to do something about it?"

Howard Hendricks says,

> Observation plus interpretation without application equals abortion. In other words, every time you observe and interpret but fail to apply, you perform an abortion on the Scriptures in terms of their purpose. The Bible was not written to satisfy your curiosity; it was written to transform your life. The ultimate goal of Bible study, then, is not to do something to the Bible, but to allow the Bible to do something to you, so truth becomes tangent to life.[1]

REVIEW

Personal Bible study begins with observation. Observation asks, What does it say? Recording observations in a notebook not only clarifies your thoughts but provides you with a lasting record of God's communication with you. Observation requires thinking, so ideally, you'll set aside a few minutes to reflect on the text, rather than just rushing through it.

After observation comes interpretation. Interpretation answers the question, What does it mean? A good interpretation is a timeless principle that reflects the point or meaning of the verse, paragraph or passage you've just read. Interpretation requires more thinking. In the process of ferreting out the underlying truths of the passage, your mind becomes saturated with biblical thinking. This is loving God with your mind.

The final step in Bible study is *application*. Application answers the question, What am I going to do about this? Application is the reason we do Bible study. From an intellectual standpoint, this is the easy step. Once you've discerned the timeless principle, applications will start popping into your brain. Rather than deep thinking, the application phase requires prayer and listening to the Spirit. The question you're praying about is, "Lord, how do you want me to apply what you've shown me in your Word?"

APPLICATION

For every timeless principle there are multiple applications. Some applications are obvious, some are not. The most important application is the one the Spirit is prompting *you* to make, which is why prayer becomes paramount during this phase. Let's look at some applications from Acts 2:41-47.

One of my observations and interpretations went like this:

Observation. In this great church the new believers were so zealous for their faith that they didn't merely attend meetings and go through motions, they *devoted* themselves to the things of the Lord (v. 42).

Principle. Church leaders should pray for and inspire devotion in their members.

What's the application?

If you're a church leader, one application would be to pray that your members catch fire for the Lord. Another would be that *you* would catch fire for the Lord. A practical step would be to decide to diligently study a portion of Scripture every morning, carry your notes with you throughout the day, and use what you recorded to share a word of encouragement with someone in every conversation you have. You might pick one or two of these, or, as you pray, you might be prompted by the Spirit to thank God that somehow you have become an inspiring leader and leave it at that.

If you're not yet a church leader, your application might be to pray for God's blessing in the lives of your leaders. Or you might begin to pray that God would make you into a leader in your church (preferably an inspiring one).

Another observation and interpretation went like this:

Observation. There was a spirit of generosity among the believers (v. 45).

Principle. Generosity is a hallmark of sincere believers.

This principle could prompt you to develop a family budget, freeing up money to give the Lord's work. If you're a student, it might prompt you to get a job so you have some means to share with others. The verse might move you to increase the percentage you give to your church. It could encourage you to give a few of your things to church members in need. I know of one family who gave their house to the church's building program as a result of this verse.

Principles are universal truths, so for every principle there are a thousand applications.

GREAT QUESTIONS

When I get to the application phase, I sometimes walk through this list of questions:

1. Is there an example for me to follow?

2. Is there a sin for me to avoid?

3. Is there a promise I can claim?

4. Is there a prayer to adapt to my situation?

5. Is there a command I need to obey?

6. Is there a verse I should memorize?

7. Is there a challenge I should take?

THE DOWNSIDE OF APPLICATION

Application is usually the place where preachers get in trouble. When a communicator explains the underlying meaning of a text, people are impressed. When the speaker gives a great illustration of the grace of God, people line up to offer their thanks. Sometimes though, when the preacher calls people to do something about the text, they accuse him of meddling in their lives. We don't like to be told that we need to change. Because of this, application-oriented teachers are sometimes called "shallow." When in fact application is the deepest form of Bible study, because improved behavior is the reason we study the Bible in the first place.

The challenge for every serious student of the Word is to make consistent application of the text. Many Christians attend church Sunday morning and a Bible study group or two throughout the week. In some traditions there's also Sunday school and a Sunday evening sermon. And there are podcasts and videocasts, and radio and television Bible teachers. In any given week, believers might find themselves drowning in biblical content, with little chance to apply all they are exposed to. The average Christian in America is learning far beyond his or her level of obedience.

THE UPSIDE OF APPLICATION

For this reason, when I record my applications I don't try to make every one of them a major change of lifestyle. Most of us don't drop forty pounds the first day we go on a diet. And few of us are able to run ten miles after spending six months on our backsides. Over time, small changes, minor course corrections, and little subtractions and additions add up to significant growth in our character and behavior. We become like Jesus one small step at a time.

A few chapters ago I mentioned that what we believe determines how we behave. Even small steps of application are significant because of the process we go through to generate them. Reading, observing and interpreting are means of loading Scripture into our mind. The more we carry God's Word and its principles in our mind, the more likely we are to do the right thing instinctively, because we're thinking the right things intellectually.

THE BEST WAY TO APPLY

Athletes in training know that the best way to make sure they get to the gym is to have a training partner or two. In community there is accountability. The best way to apply Scripture on a consistent basis is to start or join a small group of like-minded men or women. The question we end our study with should always be, What are you going to do about this? and the question we begin the next session with is always, How did you do with applying our last lesson?

ASSIGNMENT

Read Acts 2:41-47 one more time. Using the list of principles you developed in the previous chapter, write two or three applications. Then *do* them.

19

Where Can I Get Help with the Bible?

It is impossible to righteously govern the world without God and the Bible.

George Washington

◆ ◆ ◆

There's a saying in the construction trades: A workman is only as good as his tools. In some ways that's true of Bible study as well. Men and women who have cared deeply about the Bible have poured years of their lives into creating tools that can help us discover insights we would likely never have uncovered on our own.

During my senior year of high school I attended a seminar where the speaker explained the concept of tithing. I had worked a variety of jobs but never given more than five dollars at a time to my local church. The speaker's explanation of the importance of tithing and the blessing attached to it convinced me that I wanted to tithe from that day forward. His words so moved me that I decided to make up for my previous lack of tithing by donating my savings account to the church.

To make sure I wasn't doing something rash, I consulted my youth pastor about my plan. He said, "Hal, you're going to need a library someday, and so before you give, let's go to the bookstore and get you some books." We walked through the bookstore, pulling books from its shelves. By the time we were through, I had the makings of a fairly decent Bible reference library. One nice thing about Bible tools is that they never go out of style. I still use these books today.

YOUR FIRST TOOL

Your first tool, of course, is a good Bible. I recommend using one you can read easily. Compact Bibles and "pocket" versions are convenient to carry, but when you want to sit and study, use a Bible that doesn't strain your eyes.

Ideally, your Bible will have some room in its margins for you to write. Your Bible will become precious to you as you underline key words and jot notes and insights that commemorate what you've learned.

In my opinion it's essential that your primary Bible has cross-references in it. Cross references are the tiny references on the side, bottom or middle of text that point you to passages on similar topics to the one you are reading. They're a treasure trove of information! For instance, Acts 2:47 says that the people in the church in Jerusalem were "praising God and enjoying the favor of all the people." Almost every time I read that verse, one question that comes to my mind is, what were those people doing that enabled them to enjoy the favor of so many people? In my Bible, just after the word *people* I have a reference note that leads me to Romans 14:17-18.

When I turn there I find, "The kingdom of God is not a matter of eating and drinking, but of righteousness, peace and joy in the Holy Spirit, because anyone who serves Christ in this way is pleasing to God and receives human approval." By reading that, I've just discovered the way to enjoy favor with people. It's not by what I do (eating and drinking), but in how I behave. When I live with a spirit of righteousness, peace and joy, it's going to be very hard for people to dislike me.

While I'm in Romans 14:18, I see a reference note at the end of the phrase "peace and joy in the Holy Spirit." So I look it up. It points me to Galatians 5:22-23, which tells me that "the fruit of the Spirit is love, joy, peace, forbearance, kindness, goodness, faithfulness, gentleness and self-control." Now I've got a whole list of attributes I can work on as I allow the Holy Spirit to lead and transform me.

I turn back to my original reading in Acts 2:47 and finish the sentence, which reads, "the Lord added to their number daily those who were being saved." That sparks a vision in me: What if a church full of people lived in the righteousness, joy and peace of the Spirit? What if they exuded the fruits of the Spirit described in Galatians 5:22-23? Imagine how attractive a group like that would be! No doubt the Lord would be able to add to our numbers daily as well. This thought fires my desire to pray, and I end my time with the Lord asking him to create in my church a spirit of righteousness, peace and joy that will change our community.

YOUR SECOND TOOL

At present, the most popular English Bible translation is the New International Version. It holds this position because it is also one of the clearest translations available. So I recommend the NIV as a primary reading Bible.

For accuracy, the English Standard Version is the newest version on the market. The second tool in your library ought to be an ESV. Having two translations enables you to compare wording when you don't understand a text. Comparing translations will also show you different emphases you might not have noticed with just one version. Plus, now and then it's nice to read a second version just to keep your reading fresh.

One of the most useful tools you'll ever own is a study Bible. A study Bible contains all sorts of helpful reference material surrounding the text. Study Bibles give an introduction to each book of the Bible along with an outline of and vital facts about the book. Each page offers notes to help you understand the meaning of the text. Many study Bibles feature profiles of famous people in the Bible, along with maps and charts and timelines.

Study Bibles come in a variety of translations. Once you've chosen your primary Bible, consider purchasing a study Bible in a second version. Tyndale's Life Application Study Bible and Zondervan's Student Bible are two of the bestsellers because of their readability and usefulness. My suggestion is that you buy an NIV for reading and then an ESV study Bible for your second reference tool.

BIBLE STUDY TOOLS

In my personal Bible time, I read/study through a book of the Bible from start to finish. Depending on the length of the book, this can take me a day, a week or a month. Once I'm through, I prayerfully choose a new book to read and study. I try to vary the *type* of literature. If I've just completed a New Testament letter, I may move to a historic, poetic or prophetic book. If I've been in the Old Testament, I'll move to the New Testament.

My favorite. Bible study purists insist that we should first read the text of Scripture. I disagree. I'm a big picture person, so before I dive into anything, I like to know what it's all about before I begin. I turn to my favorite biblical reference book for a big picture overview. The book is called *Talk Thru the Bible*.[1] In four or five pages this gem gives me an overview of the book, when and where it was written, an outline, a key verse, its unique contribution to the Bible, and other useful information. In less than ten minutes *Talk Thru* whets my appetite and forecasts what I'm about to experience. If I could own only one study tool, this would be it.

Concordances. Once upon a time a concordance was an indispensable tool. A concordance is like an index. It lists the words of the Bible in alphabetical order. If you want to know where to find a verse on *love*, the concordance will give you a list of verses that include *love*. Many Bibles have a small concordance in the back. An *exhaustive* concordance is a concordance that lists literally *every* word in the Bible, every time it occurs. If you're going to buy a concordance, buy an exhaustive one.

The two most popular concordances today are *Young's Analytical Concordance to the Bible* and *Strong's Exhaustive Concordance of the Bible*. They're both large, so they really are exhaustive—you have to be young or strong if you're going to carry them with you.

In 1890, James L. Strong gave a number to each unique Hebrew and Greek word. So, if someone wants to know the root of that word, he or she can trace it without having to read Hebrew or Greek. And if the person wants to know if two occurrences of *love* in an English Bible are the same word in Greek, he or she can compare the numbers. Strong's numbers have been used in a variety of more advanced tools as well, so owning a *Strong's* may be the way to go.

Strong's lists every word in the chronological order it appears in the English Bible. *Young's Concordance* groups all the occurrences of a word according to its original language. When I turn to the word *love* in *Young's*, I find three Hebrew words (*ahabah, dod, rayah*) and two Greek words (*agapē* and *phileō*) and each of the places they appear as "love" in an English Bible. This can be handy if you want to know how many times the book of John uses the word *agapē* (unconditional love) versus *phileō* (brotherly love), for instance.

A few years ago, Bible Gateway (www.biblegateway.com) developed an online concordance. I still turn to my *Young's* and *Strong's* now and then, but if I'm near a computer, I find myself using Bible Gateway's version almost exclusively. Bible Gateway also has Bible dictionaries and commentaries on its site, as do other online Bible reference services. Most of these tools are older books whose copyrights have expired. If you consult them, be aware that more recent scholarship or archaeological discoveries may have made their information outdated.

Bible dictionaries. A Bible dictionary is a cross between a dictionary and an encyclopedia. Suppose I'm studying the book of 1 Corinthians and I want to know what the city of Corinth was like. I look it up and discover that it was a major trade city in the Roman Empire. It was a city of wealth and immorality. "To live like a Corinthian" meant to live a life of vice. It was the Las Vegas of its day. Now I'm beginning to understand why Paul issued so many warnings to these people! They were out of control.

Apollos helped found the Corinthian church. Suppose I don't know anything about him. I turn to "Apollos" in my Bible dictionary and learn that he was a Jew from Alexandria (a city in Africa), and that he's mentioned in Acts 18–19; 1 Corinthians 1; 3–4; 16; and Titus 3. From reading just a few paragraphs I discover that Apollos was a significant player in the early church! The dictionary says he had impressive teaching gifts. No wonder 1 Corinthians 3:3-4 says that a lot of people in Corinth preferred his teaching to that of the apostle Paul.

Bible atlases. Most Bibles have a section with maps at the back. A Bible atlas is like that section, only on steroids. A good Bible atlas provides historical, cultural and archaeological data. Many atlases are laid out chronologically. Abraham left Ur of the Chaldeans in Genesis 12. Turn to Genesis 12 in an atlas and you'll find a map of the route he took, a diagram of the topography and a discussion of the culture of his day. When I open an atlas I often find myself reading page after page of stuff I never anticipated. It's one of my favorite tools.

Commentaries. Commentaries are written by scholars who have forgotten more about the Bible than you'll ever know. Reading a commentary is like sitting down with a godly saint and letting him or her explain the Bible to you.

Commentaries are great for four things. They provide the historical context of each book and passage. They answer questions you can't figure out for yourself. They shed light on important words from the original languages. And they discuss various interpretations of a given passage. One mark of a good commentary is that it will give you all the various interpretations and their strengths and weaknesses, rather than just describing the interpretation the author favors.

A commentary can either be *exegetical*, meaning it majors on explaining the text, or *homiletical*, meaning it expounds the message of the text. Some commentaries are a blend of both. Using a homiletical commentary can be like reading a sermon—you'll receive the perspective and opinion of its author, and not just straight information about the meaning of the text. Ideally, you'll own a commentary or two on every book of the Bible, which can get expensive. I recommend you start with something like *The Expositor's Bible Commentary*, abridged edition, which is a twelve-volume work by Zondervan. At 3,136 pages, you get a lot of commentary for your money.

There are several complete sets of commentaries worth considering, including *The Expositor's Bible Commentary* (12 vols.), *The New International Commentary* (23 Old Testament vols., 18 New Testament vols.), *The Tyndale Commentaries* (28 Old Testament vols., 20 New Testament vols.), and *The Word Biblical Commentary* (59 vols.). Some of these are available on CD-ROM or for download at a greatly reduced price.

For a slightly different angle, Walton, Matthews and Chavalas have produced *The IVP Bible Background Commentary* on the Old Testament, while Craig Keener has produced *The IVP Bible Background Commentary* on the New Testament and David Stern has written *The Jewish New Testament Commentary*.

When studying a passage of Scripture, a commentary is the last tool you should turn to. Otherwise, you are reading the Bible through the lens of another, rather than letting it speak to you directly.

Other tools. When I was a little guy, I used to enjoy jumping into a swimming pool to see if I could dive down and touch the drain. I'd pinch my nose and try to avoid getting a headache as I went deeper. Then I discovered the mask and snorkel. One day, some friends invited me to Catalina Island. We brought snorkel gear and spent the day exploring the underwater life there. I was so captivated by the experience I enrolled in a scuba class. Using scuba gear, I could really go deep!

Studying the Bible can be like that. You open one tool and discover a whole new world. If you buy a few tools, you'll find deeper beauty farther underneath the waves. Some people want to go further, so they invest in equipment that will take them deeper. A few of the tools that take me deeper are

* *The Big Book of Bible Difficulties* by Norman Geisler and Thomas Howe. These two seminary professors have fielded just about every question you can imagine. If you've wondered where Cain got his wife, they'll offer you the most likely possibility. If you want to know why Matthew says there were two donkeys for Jesus' triumphal entry into Jerusalem while Mark and Luke mention one, they'll tell you. They'll answer a thousand other questions as well.

* *The Encyclopedia of Bible Characters* by Paul Gardner. There are 2,930 characters in the Bible. This book gives biographical information on most of them.

* Old Testament and New Testament surveys. These are textbooks used in Bible college and seminary classes. They give background and overview material sometimes not found in basic Bible dictionaries or commentaries. At the back of my *New Testament Survey* by Robert Gundry is a one-page chart

listing the New Testament books in chronological order, with the author, date of writing, place of writing, theme and distinctive emphasis of each book. I often turn to this book.

* *The Archaeological Study Bible* by Zondervan. This is a whole Bible that includes articles about archaeological discoveries that shed light on Scripture.

* *How to Read the Bible for All Its Worth* by Gordon Fee and Douglas Stuart. Each type of literature in the Bible requires a slightly different interpretive approach. Fee and Stuart give practical help on how to study the Epistles, narratives, Gospels, parables, the Law, the Prophets, the Psalms, wisdom literature and the book of Revelation.

RECOMMENDATION

Textbooks are expensive. In the past twenty years I have yet to pay full price for any of these resources. Most of them can be purchased for fifteen to forty dollars on websites like Amazon.com or ChristianBooks.com. I recommend you buy one tool at a time and enjoy it like you would a new article of clothing. Read the opening pages, which will explain how to get the most out of the book. Explore it with excitement and enthusiasm before making your next buy.

ASSIGNMENT

Read 2 Timothy 4:9-13. Paul is writing this letter to Timothy from prison in Rome. Use your skills of observation, interpretation and application. Two of the questions you want to ask are

1. Why did Paul want Timothy to bring him "my scrolls, especially the parchments"?

2. What kind of scrolls and parchments were they?

20

How Can I Master the Bible?

Do your best to present yourself to God as one approved,
a worker who does not need to be ashamed and
who correctly handles the word of truth.

The Apostle Paul, 2 Timothy 2:15

◆ ◆ ◆

Mastery means "consummate skill" or "full command of the subject." Under that definition, Michael Jordan mastered the game of basketball, Van Cliburn mastered the piano, and Bobby Fischer mastered the game of chess. For a while there it looked like Tiger Woods would master the game of golf. Maybe he still will. But nobody will ever master the Bible.

Jewish rabbis memorize the entire Old Testament, but they never master it. Some Christians have memorized the entire Bible, yet they remain students, not masters of it. The truth is, you cannot master the Bible. But it can master you.

We would be wise to let the Bible be our master. A few chapters ago we saw that Ezra studied the law of the Lord and *practiced* it (Ezra 7:10 NASB). The English Standard Version says he "set his heart to study the Law, . . . and do it." The New International Version reads, "Ezra had devoted himself to the study and observance of the

Law." The New Living Translation expresses it as, "Ezra had determined to study and obey the Law." That's the best we can do. We can *set our hearts*, we can *devote ourselves*, we can *determine* to study, but we can never master the Bible, because the Bible is the living expression of God's will for our lives, and we'll always fall short.

That's the bad news.

GOOD NEWS

The good news is, those who determine, devote and set their hearts to be mastered by this Book find themselves thinking and acting more like God and less like who they once were. That's what Moses was driving at when he said, "They are not just idle words for you—they are your life" (Deuteronomy 32:47).

It is possible for the Word of God to gain mastery over you. The apostle Paul let us in on his secret when he said that God's Word has divine power to demolish the destructive thought patterns of this world. "We demolish arguments," he said, "and every pretension that sets itself up against the knowledge of God, and we take captive every thought to make it obedient to Christ" (2 Corinthians 10:4-5). How did he do that? By saturating himself in the Word of God. Little by little he began to replace poor thought patterns with the thought patterns of God.

Not long after that, Paul encouraged his protégé Timothy to "do your best to present yourself to God as one approved, a worker who does not need to be ashamed and who correctly handles the word of truth" (2 Timothy 2:15). To Paul, it really is possible to be mastered by Scripture.

EATING THE ELEPHANT

Just about everyone knows how to eat an elephant—one bite at a time. The key to letting the Bible master us is to have a realistic plan we can stick with over the long haul.

In his book *Outliers*, Malcolm Gladwell stumbled upon an

interesting number. He quotes Daniel Levitin, author of *This Is Your Brain on Music*, as saying,

> The emerging picture . . . is that ten thousand hours of practice is required to achieve the level of mastery associated with being a world-class expert—in anything. In study after study, of composers, basketball players, fiction writers, ice skaters, concert pianists, chess players, master criminals, and what have you, this number comes up again and again. . . . No one has yet found a case in which true world-class expertise was accomplished in less time. It seems that it takes the brain this long to assimilate all that it needs to know to achieve true mastery.[1]

Just for fun, let's assume that it will take us that same ten thousand hours to have our thoughts taken captive to obedience to Christ. How much elephant would we have to eat, for how long, to achieve ten thousand hours of Bible saturation?

TEN THOUSAND HOURS

Assuming you attend a church where the songs contain biblical content and the pastor preaches the Word of God, let's count one hour for church attendance every week.

Then there's time in a small group Bible study. We all need a group of friends to do life with, so if you're not in small group today, I hope you'll join one (or start one yourself) as soon as you can. With your small group study, you can credit yourself for another hour of biblical content each week.

No one can build a relationship with God without personal time in his Word. Pastors and seminary professors devote significant chunks of time to reading and studying Scripture, but for most everyone else, a half hour is probably a realistic stretch of schedule. Leaving off Sunday and figuring that something unexpected will come up at least one of the other six days, that leaves five days of a half hour of study, which comes to two-and-a-half hours per week.

As you progress in your faith, there will come a point when you admit you have something to offer others, and you become a small group leader. Realistically, you're going to have to put in an hour or two of preparation for the Bible study you're now leading.

One hour church plus one hour small group plus two-and-a-half hours of personal time with God equals four-and-a-half hours a week. Add two hours preparation when you begin leading a Bible study. That brings you to six-and-a-half hours of Bible a week. At six-and-a-half hours a week, it will take you thirty years to reach ten thousand hours of Bible. That may seem like a long time, but when you consider that you are talking about being conformed to the image of Christ, that's not bad at all!

Now you've got a plan, or at least a benchmark. You know how much elephant you're going to have to eat in order to be mastered by the Bible in your lifetime. If you want to arrive sooner, increase your personal Bible study, or add a second preparation time by volunteering to teach Sunday school. Or enroll in a Bible class at church or on the Internet. Or go to Bible college or seminary for intensified training.

Whatever you do, make a plan. You can do this! And it will be worth it. Along the way you will find yourself increasingly viewing the world and its people through God's eyes. You'll be transforming by the renewing of your mind. You'll be wiser, smarter, more faith-filled, more hopeful. Like the people in Acts 2:47, chances are you'll be enjoying the favor of more and more people as you become a more and more godly person too.

SUGGESTIONS

1. Take advantage of holidays. If you choose to travel this ten-thousand-hour journey, you'll probably want to buy every tool I mentioned in chapter nineteen. Rome wasn't built in a day, and your library won't be either. A few years ago my daughter asked me to buy her a commentary for Christmas. I thought it was such a good idea, I've adopted it birthdays and Easter too. This not only solves my shop-a-phobia problems (one size fits all, and I can purchase online), it's building her library one holiday at a time. One of the great struggles your loved ones have is what to get you for Christmas and birthdays. You've now got a shopping list that will last you for years!

2. *Change translations.* All athletes know they have to switch exercise routines occasionally in order to stay sharp. I recommend that once or twice a year you put down your normal Bible and spend a month or so reading a different version. You'll gain new insights, and when you switch back to "old faithful," it will feel like you're coming home to an old friend.

3. *Have a balanced diet.* Given a choice, we'd all eat dessert first. A proper diet demands that we eat from every food group at every meal. As you choose which book of the Bible to study next, think through the type of literature you've been in recently and try a different kind. Over the next four or five years (if not sooner), you'll want to read every book of the Bible. Be sure you read the prophets (with help from a commentary) and wisdom literature, as well as epistles and narratives. These comprise "the whole council of God."

4. *Tell somebody what you're doing.* It can be daunting to announce to the world that you're taking on the ten-thousand-hour challenge. But if you don't articulate it to someone, there's a good chance you'll never get there. Take a week or so to think through your particular elephant-eating program, then share your plan with a trusted friend and ask him or her to check on your progress from time to time.

5. *Remember the application!* One of Satan's greatest weapons and our greatest weaknesses is *pride*. Read through Proverbs and you'll see that God dislikes pride more than he dislikes fornication. The pit of pride is easy to fall into. The Pharisees were determined to saturate themselves in the Bible. It became their life and their measuring stick. As they measured themselves against others, they liked what they saw in the mirror and felt superior to all non-Pharisees.

The way to avoid pride is to measure yourself against Jesus and Scripture rather than your neighbor. Remember, it's not how much you know but how much you're obeying that is the mark of maturity. In the long and short run, diligent application outweighs observation and interpretation combined. Major in doing what the Bible tells you to do. "Anyone who listens to the word but does not do what it says is like someone who looks at his face in a mirror and, after looking at himself, goes away and immediately forgets what he looks like" (James 1:23). Remember what you really look like in comparison to God's standards and his Son.

ASSIGNMENT

Read Isaiah 32:8, Proverbs 16:9 and Psalm 90:12.

1. What do these verses have in common?

2. What are these verses asking you to do?

3. Now read 2 Timothy 2:15. What is your application?

Small Group Study Guide

The Bible Questions was designed to be used in any of three ways:

1. as a personal tool to be read like any other book

2. as a small groups tool to be read and discussed together over a six-week period

3. as a church campaign to be read and discussed in conjunction with weekly sermons

When used in a small group or church campaign, the ideal pace is to cover one section per week. Participants will meet for six weeks of Bible study and read the five chapters of a section each week. In a church campaign, participants should coordinate their reading and Bible study with the church's preaching series. We've designed a six-week sermon series that begins with a pre-campaign message titled "What Can the Bible Do for Me?" It is designed to encourage church members to invite friends to the series and enroll in a small group. The series comprises messages corresponding to each section of the book. The final week's sermon reviews the material and answers the question, what do I do now? Manuscripts for these sermons, along with a Church Campaign guide with suggestions for ramping up for your campaign, are available at www.pastormentor.com.

THE BENEFITS OF A SMALL GROUP

"As iron sharpens iron, so one person sharpens another" (Proverbs 27:17). Small groups can have an enormous impact on your life and faith. They help build friendship and provide support, and they offer you a group of people who can encourage you and hold you accountable for your growth.

Truth be told, we retain only a small portion of what we read, something like 10 percent. That percentage doubles when we cover the same material a second time. Your small group will retrace much of the same territory you covered in your personal reading of *The Bible Questions*. You'll have a chance to discuss what you've learned with others, which will increase your learning even further. You'll also hear their thoughts, which will broaden your thinking as well.

SMALL GROUP COVENANT

For maximum benefit, it helps if you all agree on the following eight guidelines ahead of time:

1. *Confidentiality:* What's shared in the group, stays in the group.

2. *Openness:* Transparency leads to community.

3. *Respect:* Everyone has a right to his or her opinion.

4. *Priority:* I won't let other things keep me from attending.

5. *Preparedness:* I'll do the reading ahead of time. (What I put into the lesson is what I'll get out of the lesson.)

6. *Participation:* Everyone contributes to the discussion; nobody overcontributes to the discussion.

7. *Ownership:* If I see ways to improve the group, I'll suggest them to the leader.

8. *Care:* If a group member is missing, one (or all) of us will call to see how they're doing.

TIPS FOR A GREAT DISCUSSION

The discussion questions in this guide are laid out according to the Bible study method in part four: observation, interpretation and application. In the guide they appear as:

"Collecting the Facts" (observation)

"Discovering Timeless Truths" (interpretation)

"Putting It into Practice" (application)

There is also a section between "Collecting the Facts" and "Discovering Timeless Truths" called "Did You Know?" This section will give you a biography or some background information relevant to the study's topic. We've developed the Bible studies around this format to help your group members learn to study the Bible on their own once the study is over.

Each study begins with a question designed to get the group thinking about the subject of the lesson while sharing something from their personal life. The group leader will want to read the questions ahead of time, tweaking or eliminating questions that don't fit the group, and possibly adding a question or two that might be more pertinent. The "Reading Review" section is designed to give participants a chance to discuss what they've learned from that week's reading.

Your leader will want to pace the questions to fit your group's available time. Forty-five to sixty minutes should be adequate to get from "Collecting the Facts" to "Putting It into Practice." The optional "Reading Review" questions will take an additional fifteen to thirty minutes, so decide ahead of time if you want to include those.

One of the most significant aspects of group life is having members pray for each other. Do your best to allow five to ten minutes for people to share prayer requests, and five to ten minutes to sincerely pray for one another. Including "Reading Review" and a time of prayer, your group time may run close to ninety minutes.

Introductory Study

The Bible's Benefits

(This is an optional study, to be used following the sermon "What Can the Bible Do for Me?")

GETTING STARTED

1. Go around the circle and introduce yourselves. Who are you? Where do you live? What's something the group would never guess by looking at you?

2. What do you hope to get out of this group exploration of the Bible?

COLLECTING THE FACTS

Read Psalm 19

3. Psalm 19 is a song written by King David as a tribute to God for the ways he reveals himself. Verses 1-6 describe God's communication through nature, or *natural revelation*. Verses 7-11 describe God's communication through the Scripture, or *special revelation*. According to verse 1, what kind of communication is coming at us through "the heavens" and "the skies"?

4. List each of the synonyms for "communicate" that you can find in verses 2-4.

5. List each of the synonyms for Scripture that you can find in verses 7-9.

6. According to David (verses 7-11) the Bible is

perfect (v. 7a)   firm (v. 9b)

trustworthy (v. 7b)   righteous (v. 9c)

radiant (v. 8b)   precious (v. 10a)

pure (v. 9a)   sweet (v. 10b)

In what way can the words of a book be pure, trustworthy, radiant, and so on?

7. Following each adjective in verses 7-11, David lists a result or benefit that comes from the Bible. Match up the benefit with its adjective:

perfect   in keeping them is great reward

trustworthy   you are warned by them

radiant   _____ (no benefit listed)

pure   _____ (no benefit listed)

firm   _____ (no benefit listed)

righteous   endures forever

precious   gives light to the eyes

sweet   gives joy to the heart

_____   makes the wise simple

_____   refreshes the soul

DID YOU KNOW?

Some have called the stars "God's oldest testament." The Jewish historian Josephus claimed that Seth (Adam's third son) named the stars. Psalm 147:4 says that God calls them each by name.

In the late 1800s, E. W. Bullinger published *Witness of the Stars* in which he describes a kind of gospel witness seen in the twelve zodiac constellations.[1] The constellations begin with the virgin and end with the lion. Some think God arranged these as a visual reminder before the Word of God was ever recorded. Since the Babylonian era, whatever message God may intend through constellations has been corrupted with astrology. Still, it's interesting to see how nature reflects God's glory, and how many of nature's wonders can remind you that God is alive and well and communicating every second of the day.

DISCOVERING TIMELESS TRUTHS

8. What does it tell you about God, his nature and his relationship to humans that he is constantly communicating with us?

9. Based on the adjectives and results David describes in verses 7-11, what do you think his experience with the Bible was like?

PUTTING IT INTO PRACTICE

10. When you read the adjectives and their results, how does it make you feel about the Bible? What does it cause you to want to do with it?

11. Are there some people you'd like to invite to join this study? If so, who, and when will you invite them?

12. How can this group be of help to each other over the next few weeks?

PRAY FOR EACH OTHER

Study 1

Inspired

(If you are participating in the sermon series, this study should be done following the "How Is the Bible Different from Other Books?" sermon.)

GETTING STARTED

1. According to *Webster's Dictionary* *inspire* means "to exert an animating, enlivening or exalting influence on." Tell the group about a time when someone inspired you.

2. The Greek word for *inspire* is *theopneustos*. It means "breathed into by God." From your understanding, how is God-breathed inspiration different than an inspiring performance or an inspiring person?

COLLECTING THE FACTS

Read 2 Timothy 3:14-17

3. What are the four ways the Bible's inspiration is profitable for people?

4. What might it be like to be rebuked or corrected by Scripture? Give a personal example if you can think of one.

5. Do you think it's possible for a person to grow to the point of being "equipped for every good work" (v. 17)? If so, what would that look like?

Read 2 Peter 1:16-21

6. Peter says we would do well to pay attention to the words of

the prophets (v. 19). Then he compares their words to "light shining in a dark place." How does this phrase help you understand the nature of biblical inspiration?

7. Who initiated prophecy, and how did it happen (vv. 20-21)?

DID YOU KNOW?

Jeremiah was a prophet who regularly wished for a different job. In Jeremiah 20, he describes the downside of being a channel for God's message:

> You deceived me, LORD, and I was deceived;
>   you overpowered me and prevailed.
> I am ridiculed all day long;
>   everyone mocks me.
> Whenever I speak, I cry out
>   proclaiming violence and destruction.
> So the word of the LORD has brought me
>   insult and reproach all day long. (Jeremiah 20:7-8)

Jeremiah didn't like being ridiculed, so he decided to stop speaking for the Lord. He resolved to keep his mouth shut whenever God gave him a revelation. It didn't work:

> But if I say, "I will not mention his word
>   or speak anymore in his name,"
> his word is in my heart like a fire,
>   a fire shut up in my bones.
> I am weary of holding it in;
>   indeed, I cannot. (Jeremiah 20:9)

8. How was Jeremiah's experience with divine revelation similar to what Peter described in 2 Peter 1:20-21?

DISCOVERING TIMELESS TRUTHS

9. What difference does it make to you that the words of Scripture are *theopneustos* (breathed into by God) rather than just words written by impressive people?

10. What should you expect to experience every time you read or study a passage of Scripture?

PUTTING IT INTO PRACTICE

11. If Scripture really can train you to the point where you will be "equipped for every good work," what would you like it to equip you for this week?

12. What will you need to do, read or study these next seven days in order to let Scripture equip you in this way?

READING REVIEW (TIME PERMITTING)

13. Looking over chapter one, what did you learn about the Bible or the authorship of the Bible that you'd like to remember?

14. According to Peter Stoner (chap. 2), what are the chances that the Bible's fulfilled prophecies are coincidence?

15. List the five marks of canonicity (chap. 3).

16. What is Codex Sinaiticus (chap. 4) and why is it important?

17. Who were the Talmudists and Masoretes (chap. 4), and what contribution did they make to the Old Testament?

18. What happened at Qumran (chap. 4), and what difference does it make to our understanding of the reliability of Scripture?

PRAY FOR EACH OTHER

Study 2

Improved

(If you are participating in the sermon series, this study should be done following the "Can the Bible Make Me Better?" sermon.)

GETTING STARTED

1. One way manufacturers try to keep your business is by continuously improving their products. Everything from toothpastes to breakfast cereals and cell phones to cars are improved at least annually. What's the latest product you've seen that was "new and improved"?

COLLECTING THE FACTS

Read Romans 12:1-3

2. In the Old Testament, a bull, lamb or ram would be killed and then placed on the altar to burn as a sacrifice to the Lord. God wants us to be living sacrifices. How do you make a *living* sacrifice?

3. What is the key to stopping you from conforming to the culture around you?

4. According to this passage, your motivation for transformation is *God's mercy*. Paul spends the first eleven chapters of Romans describing God's mercy. What do you understand God's mercy to be?

5. How are we supposed to think of ourselves?
Is that easy or hard for you?

Read Romans 12:9-21

6. There are over twenty-five commands in this section of Scripture. Tell us about one command you are improving in, and one you need to improve in.

7. Why does Paul start with "the renewing of your mind" (v. 2) before he lists all these behaviors (vv. 9-21) we're supposed to follow?

DID YOU KNOW?

Haddon Robinson is a seminary professor who has spent his life teaching men and women to appreciate the Bible and be transformed by it. Robinson is a godly man. But you wouldn't have guessed it from his beginnings.

Haddon was raised in Harlem, New York City. His family lived in a section of the city called "Mouse Town." Life was hard. Gangs were prevalent. As a child Haddon learned rough ways and rough language on the streets. He met Christ in his teen years and everything began to change. *Slowly.* God's Word transforms people miraculously, but its work is most often slow and steady; one step, one sanded rough edge, one improvement of character at a time.

8. How do you explain the transformation that has taken place in Haddon Robinson and people like him?

9. Robinson never actually joined a gang. But do you think it's possible for everyone to move from gang member to world-renowned Bible teacher? Why or why not?

DISCOVERING TIMELESS TRUTHS

10. What is pleasing to God about a living sacrifice?

11. What is the principle underlying Romans 12:2? See if you can put it into a memorable statement or motto that the group can memorize.

PUTTING IT INTO PRACTICE

12. Share with the group what it would take for you to live the next twenty-four hours as a living sacrifice.

13. What would it take for you to have your mind significantly renewed in the next twenty-four hours?

14. Share with the group which of the two previous questions you'll try to apply over the next twenty-four hours. Journal about it afterward (in less than half a page) and bring your journal to share next week.

READING REVIEW (TIME PERMITTING)

15. From chapter seven, what is the purpose of the Bible?

16. Chapter eight states, "Most of the significant battles we face take place inside our mind." Do you agree or disagree with that? Why?

17. What keeps you from reading the Bible daily? What would be your ideal pattern of Bible reading?

18. Look back at chapter ten and complete the theme of the Bible here:

    God is building a _____.

PRAY FOR EACH OTHER

Study 3

God's Name

(If you are participating in the sermon series, this study should be done following the "Answering Your Bible Questions—Live" presentation.)

GETTING STARTED

1. If you brought your journal from last week's exercise, read what you wrote about living as a sacrifice or having your mind renewed. If you didn't bring your journal, describe your experience from memory.

2. What is your full name?

COLLECTING FACTS

Read Exodus 33:12–34:8

3. What prompted God to share his full name with Moses?

4. Moses asked to see God's *glory* (Exodus 33:18). The Lord responded by showing him his *goodness* (v. 19). What's the difference between God's goodness and his glory? What is it about God's glory that made it impossible for Moses to behold?

5. How long does God's love continue compared to the length of his wrath?

6. God's great name represents his essence and character. He describes himself with eight characteristics:

    1. compassionate
    2. gracious

3. slow to anger
4. abounding in love and faithfulness
5. maintaining love to thousands
6. forgiving wickedness, rebellion and sin
7. does not leave the guilty unpunished
8. punishes the children and their children to the third and
   fourth generation

What's the balance here between love and grace, and justice and holiness?

7. How does Moses respond to this revelation of God's love and character (v. 8)?

DID YOU KNOW?

God's name and characteristics are essentially repeated in Numbers 14:18; 2 Chronicles 30:9; Nehemiah 9:17; Psalm 86:15; 111:4; 116:5; 145:8; Joel 2:13; Jonah 4:2; Nahum 1:3.

• In Numbers 14, the Israelites refuse to enter the Promised Land. God threatens to destroy them. Moses reminds the Lord of his great name, and God relents and forgives them.

• In 2 Chronicles 30, King Hezekiah sends an invitation to all Israel to join him for Passover. He reminds them of God's great name as incentive for them to come celebrate.

• In Nehemiah 9, Ezra reads the law to the people and then re-cites God's characteristics as he worships the Lord in prayer.

• In Psalm 86, David is facing opposition from his enemies. He appeals to God, asking him for mercy, salvation and comfort.

• In Psalms 111, 113 and 145 the psalmist praises God's great name.

• In Psalm 116, the psalmist records his thanksgiving, testifying to God's great name and how good he has been.

• In Joel 2, the prophet calls the people to repentance, assuring them of the Lord's gracious character by recounting God's great name.

- In Jonah 4, Jonah laments that God has relented from sending calamity on Nineveh. The prophet admits that he didn't want to call the Ninevites to repentance because he knew God's great name would cause them to relent and turn from their wickedness.

- In Nahum 1, Nahum uses God's character as part of his proof that one day God will destroy Nineveh, which he did 150 years later.

8. Thinking through these passages, what does knowing God's great name and character do for the Israelites? In what kinds of situations does it give them courage and hope?

DISCOVERING TIMELESS TRUTHS

9. What does God's name tell you about his feelings toward people's sin?

10. What does his name tell you about his response to your repentance?

11. How does God's name explain what you see happening in our world today?

PUTTING IT INTO PRACTICE

12. How hard would it be for you to memorize God's great name and characteristics (Exodus 34:6-7)?

13. What would it do for your mind and heart if you did memorize it?

14. Are you willing, as a group, to memorize Exodus 34:6-7 this week? (Hints: Write it out multiple times so that you see it, say it and feel it while committing it to memory. Learn it phrase by phrase. Write it on a three by five card, pull it out, and recite it two or three times a day for the next week. Come back ready to share with the group.)

READING REVIEW (TIME PERMITTING)

15. From chapter eleven, what are the advantages of having multiple translations of the Bible?

16. Do you think Christianity is too narrow? If you were God, what means would you design for humans to become your friends? What would you do to establish love and maintain justice at the same time?

17. Why do you think the Lord has left the timing of Jesus' return ambiguous in Scripture?

18. The Trinity is a hard concept to define, and harder still to understand. What questions do you have about God's three-in-one-ness?

PRAY FOR EACH OTHER

Study 4

Mastered

(If you are participating in the sermon series, this study should be done following the "How Can I Master the Bible?" sermon.)

GETTING STARTED

1. How well did you do memorizing Exodus 34:6-7? Go around the circle and recite as much of it as you can.

2. What skill, hobby or endeavor have you spent the most time on over the past few years?

COLLECTING THE FACTS

3. Read 2 Timothy 2:15. What might it look like to "do your best" to become someone who handles the Word of God well?

4. Currently, how well do you handle God's Word? Explain.

5. Read Isaiah 32:8. What is noble about putting effort into being mastered by Scripture?

6. Read Proverbs 16:9. What sort of plan do you or would you like to have for being mastered by Scripture?

7. Read Psalm 90:10, 12. If you live to be ninety, approximately how many days do you have left to gain wisdom?

DID YOU KNOW?

In the early 1990s psychologists studied violin students at the elite Academy of Music in Berlin. They divided the students into categories of "world class," "good" and "future music teacher." Each student was asked, "How many hours have you practiced?" The future music teachers had logged four thousand hours on their instruments. The good musicians had logged eight thousand. The world-class violinists had each logged ten thousand hours.

In his book *Outliers*, Malcolm Gladwell notes that the striking thing about this study is that no "natural" musicians were found in any of the groups. All the greats practiced thirty or more hours a week. Likewise, there were no "no talent" players who had simply ground out enough practice to become proficient. Every one of these violinists had achieved their respective levels through a combination of talent and hard work. Average musicians work an average amount, good musicians work a goodly amount, and great musicians work a great amount.

The Beatles formed their band in 1957. In 1960, they were invited to play in the all-night strip clubs of Hamburg, Germany. Up till then, they had been playing one hour gigs several nights a week. The Hamburg clubs had them playing eight hours at a stretch. During that three-year period, the Beatles' live onstage performances exceeded two thousand hours of performance time—more than most bands play in their entire careers. Great musicians become great because of the great amount of time they spend on their discipline.

The magic number for world-class proficiency in almost anything—hockey, chess, computer programming, violin and rock 'n' roll—seems to be ten thousand hours. Gladwell says, "It seems that it takes the brain this long to assimilate all that it needs to know to achieve true mastery."[2]

8. How well do you know the Bible? Explain.

9. How well would you like to know the Bible? What are you going to do about this?

DISCOVERING TIMELESS TRUTHS

10. Read 2 Timothy 2:15. What is Paul asking serious Christians to do?

11. What would it look like to do that in your life?

12. What would you need to start doing to accomplish that?

13. What would you need to stop doing to accomplish that?

PUTTING IT INTO PRACTICE

14. What one small step would you like to take toward allowing the Bible to master you in the next three months?

15. How can the group help you start and sustain that step?

READING REVIEW (TIME PERMITTING)

16. Do you have any questions the rest of us can help you with in the *observation*, *interpretation* and *application* process? If so, what are they?

17. What Bible reference tools do you hope to buy over the next few years?

PRAY FOR EACH OTHER

Study 5

Living Scripture

(If you are participating in the sermon series, this study should be done following the "How Do I Live What I've Learned?" sermon.)

GETTING STARTED

1. Now that the book reading is completed, how are you doing with practicing observation, interpretation and application in your personal Bible study times?

2. Share an insight or two you've gleaned from your study this week.

COLLECTING THE FACTS

Read Deuteronomy 6:1-9

3. According to verse 2, what's the secret to a long life?

4. According to verse 3, what two actions should Israel practice so that things will go well and they will increase?

5. According to verse 5, we are to love God with everything we have. What does verse 6 say we must do in order for that to be possible?

6. Verses 7-9 list four behaviors that will put God's Word into your heart. What are they? And what might these practices look like in our twenty-first-century world?

DID YOU KNOW?

Deuteronomy 6:4-5 is one of the most sacred texts in all of Judaism. The verse begins with the Hebrew word *Shema*, meaning "Hear," and proclaims the nature of God (which is *ehad* or "oneness"). It explains how to respond to God's oneness (which is by loving him with everything you have). Many Jews recite the *Shema* every morning and evening. This passage is a way Jews dedicate their hearts and souls to God together as they begin certain meetings. In Reformed and Conservative congregations, the Rabbi or meeting-convener will invite everyone to stand and "say *Shema.*" They stand out of respect for these sacred words. In Orthodox congregations, they do just the opposite: they sit out of respect for the words. Either way, the people recite *Shema* in full voice, in Hebrew together. It's one of those rituals that unifies a people.

For fun, your group might want to recite the *Shema* in English together (in full voice).

DISCOVERING TIMELESS TRUTHS

7. What does the *Shema* tell you about God, his nature and how he wants you to relate to him?

8. What timeless principles do you see in this passage that can affect how you practice letting the Bible master you? Everyone should describe at least one practice. If time permits, ask everyone to share a second practice as well.

PUTTING IT INTO PRACTICE

9. What have you learned during *The Bible Questions?*

10. How will you live differently as a result of this study?

11. As you end *The Bible Questions*, decide as a group whether to continue meeting together for Bible study, and if so, what the group will study together and for how long.

PRAY FOR EACH OTHER

Acknowledgments

Every time I write a book I rediscover that it is impossible to do anything truly worthwhile by myself. The folks at InterVarsity Press took my work and vastly improved it. Special thanks to Dave Zimmerman for your coordinating and writing abilities. Also to Drew Blankman (the content reader) for catching several errors before they ever went into print, as well as to Jeanna Wiggins (book layout) for making these words readable. Deborah Saenz Gonzalez, Jeff Crosby and Nathan Baker-Lutz, you were a joy to work with. Thanks to you all!

Don Otis (Veritas Communications), you continue to be a blessing to me by arranging engaging interviews all over the country.

From my own staff, Jim Britts, Frank Cortes, Ken Lippold, Jan Nelson and Ben Tabbal—you all have treated this work as an extension of your own ministry and worked diligently to enable other churches to benefit from it. I love you guys! Frank, Ken and my own daughter, Amy Seed, have helped me so much with creative ideas for connecting with churches and their surrounding communities. I am more than grateful.

The staff of Outreach, Inc., has been immensely helpful by creating invitational tools. Scott Evans, Steve Foster and Brian Orme, you are stars in the marketing world.

I also want to thank New Song's Leadership Board: Mark Williams, Cynthia Standley, Sandy O'Connell, Anthony Biondo, Emil Reyes and Chuck Riffe, for affording me time to write and serve those outside our church. I love doing life with you!

Appendix 1

The Bible Study Process

Observation = What does the text say?
Interpretation = What does the text mean? (timeless principles)
Application = What should I do about it?

OBSERVATION QUESTIONS

1. Who is mentioned in this passage?

2. Who is the main character of this passage?

3. What happens in this passage?

4. What must I know to understand this passage?

5. When did this happen? (Is time important in the passage?)

6. Where did this happen? (Is location or geography important to the passage?)

7. How did this happen?

8. How many people are involved?

9. How does God enter into this?

10. Why did this happen?

11. Why did the characters do what they did?

12. Why did God include this in his Word?

13. What else is important to note about this passage?

INTERPRETATION QUESTIONS

1. What's the point being made in this observation?

2. In what way is this observation true today?

3. In what way is this observation true in my cultural setting?

State what you believe is a principle that flows from this passage or observation. Once you've developed a principle, answer the following:

1. Does this principle seem true to what God is saying in this passage?

2. Does it seem true to what God teaches elsewhere in Scripture?

3. Is this principle almost always true?

4. Is this principle a way of seeing the world or doing life that is in conformity to God's ways?

APPLICATION QUESTION

Of all the ways I could apply these principles, Lord, what do you most want me to do about it today?

Appendix 2

The Bible in One Verse

The Bible's message and purpose is summarized in Romans 6:23: "For the wages of sin is death, but the gift of God is eternal life in Christ Jesus our Lord."

Six simple words summarize God's message to the world:

1. *Wages.* Wages are what we get paid for the work we perform.

2. *Sin.* While it sounds like a terrible word, *sin* (*harmartia*) is an archery term that means "to miss the mark."

3. *Death.* Many people think of death as the end of all things. The Bible indicates that death is the beginning of a new stage of life. It's a separation of our body from our soul. Everyone will live somewhere for all of eternity. Either with God, or away from God. In fact, at the resurrection you'll receive a new body.

4. *Gift.* A gift is the opposite of a wage. A gift can't be earned, only accepted.

5. *God.* God is the perfect Creator of the universe. The challenge for us is, how can imperfect humans reach a perfect God?

6. *Life.* The "life" spoken about here is "eternal life in Christ Jesus." This is the gift available to those who will accept it.

The Bible says that all of us have sinned. We've done things that were less than perfect, which means we've fallen short of God. Many religions design ways for people to work off their imperfection by doing acts of goodness. The problem is, doing good things doesn't make us perfect. If I miss the first question on a test, I can get all the rest of the answers right, and I'll still have a less-than-perfect score.

God knew we couldn't work our way to perfection, so he made another way. Instead of asking us to become perfect, he sent his Son to be perfect on our behalf. Jesus Christ lived a perfect life. He never sinned, so he never incurred the death penalty for his wages. Instead, he offered his perfect life in exchange for our sin-scarred lives. Imagine a judge sentencing you to prison for a crime you've committed. Imagine you're guilty, and you know it. Jesus steps forward and offers to serve your sentence for you. That's what his life was all about.

In Genesis 3 our first parents did the one thing God asked them not to do. We've been doing things we know we shouldn't ever since. In order to rescue us, God sent his Son to pay the penalty for our sins. His only condition is that we would admit we have sinned and receive the forgiveness Jesus offers, and then turn and follow him as Lord.

The wages of sin is death. We deserved separation from God because of our sin. But God doesn't want us to experience eternal separation, he wants us to be with him forever. Instead of enforcing justice, God offers us mercy through Christ.

The gift of God is eternal life in Christ Jesus our Lord. If you would like to receive this gift of eternal life, pray this prayer:

> Lord Jesus, I admit that I have sinned. I have done things that I knew were wrong, and I ask your forgiveness. I invite you now to be my Savior and my Lord. Since my life now belongs to you, I purpose to follow you from now on. I will do my best to do what you ask me to do and live the way you ask me to live. In Jesus' name, amen.

If you prayed that prayer, tell someone. Get in a Bible-believing church, where others can help you take steps in your new relationship with Christ.

TWO PROMISES

Here are two promises for you:

- "God has given us eternal life, and this life is in his Son. Whoever has the Son has life; whoever does not have the Son of God does not have life" (1 John 5:11-12). If you prayed the previous prayer and meant it, you have the Son. Which means that you now have life!

- "If anyone is in Christ, the new creation has come: The old has gone, the new is here!" (2 Corinthians 5:17). If you prayed the prayer and meant it, you are *in Christ.* Which means that you are starting a brand new life! Live it well, for him!

Notes

Chapter 1: Who Wrote the Bible?

[1]If you'd like more on this, see Hal Seed, *The God Questions* (Vista, Calif.: Outreach, 2009), p. 39.

[2]These writing prophets and their books are mentioned in 1 Chronicles 29:29; 2 Chronicles 9:29; 13:22; 20:34; 32:32; 33:19.

[3]These books are mentioned in 1 Kings 11:41; 14:19; 14:29; 15:7 (ESV).

[4]Ezra probably used "the book of the kings of Israel," "the annals of King David"; "the records of Samuel the seer, the records of Nathan the prophet, and the records of Gad"; "the prophecy of Ahijah the Shilonite," "the visions of Iddo the seer"; "the records of Shemaiah the prophet"; "the book of the kings of Judah and Israel"; "the vision of the prophet Isaiah"; "the annals of Jehu," "the writings of David and his son Solomon," and other books available at that time. These books are mentioned in 1 Chronicles 9:1; 27:24; 29:29; 2 Chronicles 9:29; 12:15; 13:22; 16:11; 20:34; 24:27; 25:26; 27:7; 28:26; 32:32; 33:19; 35:4; 35:27; 36:8.

[5]The following are attested to David: Psalm 3–9; 11–32; 34–41; 51–65; 68–70; 86; 101; 103; 108–110; 122; 124; 131; 133; 138–145. Acts 4:25 credits David with writing Psalm 2, and Hebrews 4:7 indicates he wrote Psalm 95.

Chapter 2: How Is the Bible Different from Other Books?

[1]J. M. Roberts, *History of the World* (New York: Oxford University Press, 1993), p. 431.

[2]Bruce Olson, *Bruchko* (Carol Stream, Ill.: Creation House, 1980), p. 121.

[3]Ibid., pp. 139-40.

[4]You can find more on Biblica's website at www.biblica.com/about-us/fact-sheet.

[5]J. Barton Payne, *Encyclopedia of Biblical Prophecy* (New York: Harper & Row, 1973).

[6]Hal Seed, *The God Questions* (Vista, Calif.: Outreach, 2009), p. 66.

[7]Hal Seed, *Future History: Understanding the Book of Daniel and End Times Prophecy* (Torrance, Calif.: New Song Press, 2007), pp. 144-55.

[8]The number is taken from Donald Campbell, *Daniel: God's Man in a Secular Society* (Grand Rapids: Discovery House, 1988), p. 162.

Chapter 3: Who Decided What Went into the Bible?

[1]Bruce Shelley, *Church History in Plain Language* (Waco, Tex.: Word, 1982), p. 72.

[2]Ibid., p. 77.

[3]I am indebted to Norman Geisler for the wording of the five questions of canonicity. See Norman Geisler, "The Canonicity of the Bible," *John Ankerberg Show*, www.ankerberg.com/Articles/historical-Jesus/DaVinci/PDF/The-Canonicity-of-the-Bible.pdf.

Chapter 4: How Accurate Is the Bible?

[1]Juan Garcés's complete description, along with some video of the Codex, can be found at the British Library's online gallery at www.bl.uk/onlinegallery/sacred texts/podjuangarces.html.

[2]For a chart of the eight most reliable documents in history, see Hal Seed, *The God Questions* (Vista, Calif.: Outreach, 2009), p. 59.

[3]This is an abbreviated description. For complete details, see Josh McDowell, *A Ready Defense* (Nashville: Thomas Nelson, 1993), p. 49.

[4]Gleason Archer, quoted in Norman Geisler and William Nix, *A General Introduction to the Bible* (Chicago: Moody, 1986), p. 367.

[5]Geisler and Nix, *A General Introduction to the Bible*, p. 263.

Chapter 5: Did God Really Write the Bible?

[1]See Don Richardson, *Eternity in Their Hearts* (Ventura, Calif.: Regal, 1985), pp. 85-104.

[2]Charles Wesley, cited in Josh McDowell, *A Ready Defense* (Nashville: Thomas Nelson, 1993), p. 178.

Chapter 7: What's the Bible's Purpose?

[1]Don Richardson, *Eternity in Their Hearts* (Ventura, Calif.: Regal, 1981), pp. 73-97.

Chapter 8: Can the Bible Make Me a Better Person?

[1]To learn how to memorize Scripture, I recommend *The Topical Memory System* by the Navigators. It will start you on a lifetime of great Scripture memory habits.

Chapter 9: What's the Central Message of the Bible?

[1]I am grateful to Bill Hybels, senior pastor of Willow Creek Community Church, for introducing me to the continuity between the three parables, and to Kenneth Bailey, *Poet and Peasant and Through Peasant Eyes,* combined ed. (Grand Rapids: Eerdmans, 1983), chap. 7, for many of the insights I have gleaned about the prodigal Father.

[2]Kenneth Bailey developed this outline in his *Poet and Peasant* (Grand Rapids: Eerdemans, 1976), p. 160.

[3]Ibid., p. 192.

Chapter 10: What's the Bible's Story Line?

[1]I am indebted to Jim Dethmer, former teaching pastor at Willow Creek Community Church, for the wording of this theme.

[2]Walter Kaiser, *The Expositor's Bible Commentary*, vol. 2 (Grand Rapids: Zondervan, 1990), p. 379.

Chapter 11: Why Are There So Many Translations?

[1]Augustine, Letter LXXXII, *Nicene and Post-Nicene Fathers*, series 1 (Grand Rapids, Eerdmans: 1983), 1:361.

Chapter 12: Why Was God So Violent in the Old Testament?

[1]Jesus refers to God as "the God of Abraham" in Luke 20:37. So did Paul (Galatians

3:8), Peter (Acts 3:13) and John the Baptist (Matthew 3:9).

Chapter 14: When Will Jesus Return?

[1]Doctrines and Covenants, sec. 130, v. 15.

[2]Yom T'ruah is described by Moses in Leviticus 23:23-25.

[3]I am indebted to my friend Dr. Les Breitman for this insight into Jewish tradition. Les is a converted Jew and member of my congregation.

[4]If you'd like to watch the gospel being preached to the whole world, go to www .greatcommission2020.com, where people inquire and come to Christ, via the Internet, on a second-by-second basis.

Chapter 15: Where Is the Trinity Found in Scripture?

[1]Arian Christianity is practiced today by the Jehovah's Witnesses and other sects, who cite Arius as one of their great doctrinal inspirations.

[2]The Trinity is such an important doctrine that words must be chosen carefully when describing it. Bruce Shelley does a very good job of this in his *Church History in Plain Language* (Waco, Tex.: Word, 1982), pp. 116-21.

Chapter 16: How Do I Study the Bible?

[1]Rudyard Kipling, "The Elephant's Child," in *Just So Stories* (New York: Macmillan, 1902).

[2]The full story can be found at <www.intervarsity.org/mx/item/4503/>.

Chapter 18: How Do I Apply What I Learn?

[1]Howard Hendricks, *Living by the Book* (Chicago: Moody Press, 1991), p. 284. Dr. Hendricks is a master of Bible study methods.

Chapter 19: Where Can I Get Help with the Bible?

[1]Bruce Wilkinson and Larry Boa, *Talk Thru the Bible* (Nashville: Thomas Nelson, 1983).

Chapter 20: How Can I Master the Bible?

[1]Daniel Levitin, *This Is Your Brain on Music: The Science of Human Obsession* (Cambridge: Cambridge University Press, 1999), p. 3, cited in Malcolm Gladwell, *Outliers: The Story of Success* (New York: Little, Brown, 2008), p. 49.

Small Group Study Guide

[1]E. W. Bullinger, *Witness of the Stars* (Grand Rapids: Kregel, 1967).

[2]Malcolm Gladwell, *Outliers* (New York: Little, Brown, 2008), p. 40.

About the Author

Hal and his wife, Lori, founded New Song Community Church in Oceanside, California, in 1992. New Song has seen over five thousand people come to Christ, planted six new churches and helped found four parachurch ministries. Hal travels to assist churches with evangelism, outreach and military ministry. He is a Walk Thru the Bible instructor and a trainer for Dynamic Church Planting International. Hal holds degrees in biblical studies and Christian education, theology and leadership.

OTHER BOOKS BY HAL SEED

The God Questions
"This book is packed with valuable information that will help skeptics believe and struggling Christians to grow stronger."
Craig Groeschel, founding pastor of LifeChurch.tv
Also available in gift and booklet editions.

Future History: Understanding the Book of Daniel and End-Times Prophecy
"*Future History* not only helps you understand what's coming, but its principles for living will help you live a better life now."
Scott Evans, founder and president of Outreach, Inc.

Jonah: Responding to God in All the Right Ways
This book will enrich your time with God, help you understand the twin peaks of his character, lead you in a daily response to his greatness and motivate you to want to serve him more fully.

For more on Hal Seed and his writing, visit halseedbooks.com or pastormentor.com.